SIGNS AND OMENS

Also by Bruce Forester

In Strict Confidence

Bruce Forester

SIGNS AND OMENS

A Novel of Suspense

DODD, MEAD & COMPANY

NEW YORK

Copyright © 1984 by Bruce Forester
All rights reserved
No part of this book may be reproduced in any form
without permission in writing from the publisher.
Published by Dodd, Mead & Company, Inc.
79 Madison Avenue, New York, N.Y. 10016
Distributed in Canada by
McClelland and Stewart Limited, Toronto
Manufactured in the United States of America
First Edition
Library of Congress Cataloging in Publication Data

Forester, Bruce.
Signs and omens.

I. Title.
PS3556.7249S5   1984   813'.54   84-8079
ISBN 0-396-08392-7

To Bernard and Leon
Gone but not forgotten

Part One

One

MANY DIFFERENT WAYS TO CHOOSE! WHICH PATH would he take? How would he do it? His eyes scanned the spacious room, past his collection of guns set out in an orderly arrangement in a cabinet Kate Robins had especially designed for his valued possessions.

He knew when he awoke this morning he could no longer postpone the inevitable. Today had to be the day. The only unresolved factor was how he'd do it. Now he knew.

He made his way past the steel desk resting under a large bay window that framed the greenery of the park below. God, how austere the room looked in comparison.

He had to maintain his motivation.

He set his stereo to the final scene of Verdi's *Otello,* turned up the volume and as he heard, *"s' anco armato mi vede. Ecco la fine del mio cammin Otello fu,"* he bolted past the two Chippendale chairs at the far corner of the room, the muscular tension in his body soaring as Otello plunged the sword into his stomach.

He raced to the bathroom, opened the medicine cabinet, and focused on the neatly arranged contents. His eyes widened as he spotted the container of razor blades partially hidden by a half-empty bottle of Eau Sauvage. He hastily reached for the thin sharp objects, knocking the cologne against the marble sink, the glass bursting apart, splashing its contents and spreading glittering fragments over the tiled floor. He grasped a razor blade and felt for his radial pulse. A wave of nausea swept over him. He couldn't slash his wrists. He'd never been able to stand the blood, the mess. Even in death he demanded meticulousness, a precise, easily executed, painless, and orderly exit.

He lifted his head and scanned the contents in the medicine cabinet. Of course, how simple. How obvious. How painless. Pills. The perfect solution. In a few moments his anguish would be over. He smiled with grim contentment.

He picked up the bottle of Doriden. Carefully he counted out forty and cupped them in his left hand. He slowly turned on the cold water, swallowed one pill, and began thinking of everlasting peace and the absence of suffering.

He had to admit he had picked the ideal time to complete his task. No last-minute visitor to stop his attempt—all his friends out of town, Kate Robins visiting her parents in Maine. He quickly gulped a second pill.

The years of agony would begin to lift as the sedative began working its wonders. This dreaded pain lasting a day or two at a time while he was at Yale had gradually stretched into periods lasting several months. In the past years, the pain had frequently reached unbearable levels only to miraculously subside, however briefly, and he'd convinced himself to continue.

But for the past six months, the gaping wound would not be ignored. He had tried everything. Pills. Booze. He even swallowed his pride and resorted as a last-ditch attempt at salvation to psychoanalysis for a while and then a brief return to the church, all without relief.

The intense drive that catapulted him to leadership roles in college and throughout later years and helped to keep him alive during these dreaded periods had slowly ebbed.

He swallowed a third Doriden. The phone rang. Should he answer the ring? He cursed the thought, yet couldn't dismiss it. The phone jangled again. He took another Doriden. Blasted phone, stop ringing. The noise kept reverberating through his temples. He looked at the pills, then glared at the phone hanging alongside the shower door. He found his resolve weakening. His conscientiousness was a curse, making him lift the receiver. He vowed he wouldn't allow the caller to prevent him from completing his final act.

"Mike, it's Russell. What took you so damn long to answer? I must see you immediately. It's a matter of utmost importance."

Hearing the explosive voice at the other end of the line sent ripples of tension through Anderson's angular frame. The one person whose life he valued needed him. Try as he could, he knew he'd never refuse his closest friend.

"Are you there?" Russell barked.

Anderson replied apologetically, "A little tired, but I'm here."

"I don't know what the hell is the matter with you, but you'd better pull yourself together, grab your black bag, and follow our usual procedure. I'll be expecting you within two hours."

A brief smile lifted the corners of Anderson's mouth. He looked with resigned eyes at the remaining capsules lying in his moist palm.

"Anderson, are you there? Answer me! I'm frightened. I need you."

"Relax, will you? I'll grab my things and I'll be there as soon as I can," Anderson muttered, his speech somewhat slurred. He replaced the phone in its cradle, the capsules in the bottle, staggered out of the bathroom, knocked against the Chesterfield sofa in the entrance to the living room, and slammed the front door behind him. He promised he'd dispense with Russell's problem rapidly and then resume ending his own.

The ride in the cab through the side streets of Manhattan was a blur. A sudden jolt caused by a jagged-edged pothole on the Belt Parkway passed without notice. Anderson fought back another wave of somnolence as he boarded the commuter flight and awkwardly fell into his seat. A tall dark-skinned attendant prodded him into accepting a cup of black coffee. Anderson continued drifting in and out of reality through an additional cup. As he began sipping his third, he felt the plane start its descent. He vaguely heard the captain apologizing for a twenty-minute delay due to unexpected heavy air traffic. While others groaned, Anderson smiled. Any delay would give his system the needed time to metabolize and excrete the ingested pills. In another hour he knew he would be alert and able to compensate for any lingering effects, but in his present state he was in no condition to help Russell.

Thirty minutes later, the captain received clearance and the massive bird glided smoothly to a gentle halt. The flight's serene ending was an ironic reminder of what Anderson had envisioned for himself, but that was before the urgent phone call that made him postpone his plan. Now he needed to harness all his inner resources to meet the challenge that lay ahead.

He removed his black bag from the overhead rack, threaded his way past the flight attendant who had nursed him, and, taking a final deep breath of cold air, went out into the smoldering heat, wondering what had caused John Russell to sound so frightened.

A long black sedan inched its way among the arriving passengers causing them to scatter in all directions before coming to rest alongside Anderson. The driver courteously opened the rear door.

Anderson sank into the comfortable leather seat. "Glad you

could make it." A deep husky voice pierced the silence. Startled, Anderson turned towards the stocky middle-aged man to his left. "Ragland, why are you here?" Brent Ragland was noticeably shaken. His piercing dark eyes met Anderson's brooding gaze. "Russell insisted I meet you upon your arrival."

Anderson was becoming increasingly alarmed. The three of them had been close friends since they roomed together at Yale in their senior year. Ragland began to work for Russell immediately upon graduation while Anderson had at routine intervals been summoned by John. In recent years a waiting limousine was commonplace but never during these times had Anderson recalled such urgency in his friends' voices nor had Ragland ever been at the airport to greet him.

As the two men rode in silence, broken briefly by small talk that led nowhere, Anderson felt the tension mounting, forcing his chemically induced dullness and drowsiness to recede. He glanced out his window. Two muscular young men dressed in dark blue suits waved the Cadillac through the wrought iron gates.

The excitement in seeing the beautiful sprawling lawns and the majestic Greek revival mansion looming in the distance never diminished regardless of how often he repeated his visits there.

The sun was setting over the western part of the mansion, its rays penetrating between the branches of a nearby oak tree, casting shadows on Anderson and Ragland as they entered the house through a side door.

They rapidly made their way past a large entranceway and down a tunnellike corridor, the only sounds the clicking of their shoes on the polished marble floor. Anderson felt conspicuous, as if the portraits that covered the walls were peering down on him.

Ragland led Anderson up a long winding staircase, nodding

as a familiar face passed by. At the top of the landing he suddenly halted and turned to his friend. "Mike, promise me one thing. After talking to Russell, level with me. That's all I want."

What did Ragland mean, "level with me"? Why wouldn't he? Had he not always in the past? Why not now? And what could Anderson discover that would be so important to him?

He could sense his stomach tightening as he passed Russell's bedroom and approached his office. He knocked on the heavy oak door, hesitating for a moment before slowly walking in, not at all certain he wanted his questions answered.

Anderson glanced around the small room once used by other families for guests, converted several years ago to a private office located across the hall from the master bedroom suite. It was Russell's untidy private office; stacks of file folders and briefing books covered his mahogany desk. Behind the disarray, seated in a green leatherback chair, was John Russell, his left hand resting on his phone.

He turned quickly in his chair and smiled in Anderson's direction. "My God, am I glad you could come so fast."

"You didn't give me much of a choice," Anderson replied. He was puzzled. Why the urgency? There was nothing to show any cause for alarm. Russell looked fit. Anderson marvelled at his ability to maintain his native California tan despite years spent in the Northeast.

"I don't know what it is. It's the damnedest thing. That's why I called," Russell said, rising and pacing around the room. He halted, at a loss for words, frowning at the floor. "That's what's been happening. I start and stop."

"Wait a minute. Let's start at the beginning." Anderson's face masked his confusion. "What do you mean, you start and stop?" Anderson was a good listener: silent, expressionless, enabling others to loosen their guard and open up. He realized it was the one quality that set him apart from many of his fellow physicians. His peers possessed similar diagnostic skills, but none of them had acquired the patience to wait until the patient finished describing his problems. They were always too busy, too rushed. Anderson secretly knew it was because his colleagues had lives to live while to him his patients were his life.

Russell began, "You've known me long enough to know I'm not the type who worries about things. If I was, I never would have gotten as far as I have. I trust you. I can't say that about most of those around me. You've been my private doctor for years. To come to the point, I'm afraid I have a serious medical problem and I don't know where else to turn. I have a lot of very important work to do and I don't know if I'm going to have the time to do it."

"Wait a minute. Stop being so melodramatic. I'm sure it can't be as serious as you think," Anderson replied, removing the sphygmomanometer and stethoscope from his black bag, "but go on, I don't mean to interrupt."

"I think it all started about three months ago. Peg had the flu and I must have caught the same bug. Anyway, I called McCormick. He examined me, told me to lighten my workload for a couple of days and I would be as good as new. The days stretched into weeks and I continued feeling worn out. More than that, I started feeling dull and apathetic. I was back to my normal work routine, but it took a tremendous effort to get through each day."

"What was McCormick's opinion?"

"He assured me that my symptoms were all normal aftermaths of the flu and if I took it easier I would recover faster."

"I take it you weren't satisfied with that advice?"

"No, it wasn't that at all. I cut back but instead of gradually feeling stronger, I sensed I was still slipping. Don't get me wrong, Art's a good doctor, but he is not you."

"Look, we've been through this before. You know why I

wanted it this way, now please continue and try to be more specific," Anderson prodded.

"That's part of the problem. I can't pinpoint what I mean. I begin to speak, as I mentioned before, and for no reason stop in midsentence."

"What else have you noticed?" Anderson asked as he wrapped the sphygmomanometer around Russell's muscular right arm.

"At times I lose track of conversations."

"For instance?" Anderson queried, trying to hide his increasing concern.

"The reason I finally decided to call you was because Ragland briefed me on an important issue early this morning but when he called three hours later and asked if I had formulated my opinion, I had no idea what in hell he was talking about. I had completely forgotten our discussion. Do you see what I'm driving at?"

"Calm down, will you? You're always preaching against people who come to premature conclusions. Does McCormick know about these concerns?"

"I've mentioned them to him, including one I forgot to tell you about. It sounds trivial, but it bothered me. I was in the middle of writing a letter when I was interrupted by my secretary. When I went back to the letter, I looked down, saw the pen lying alongside the paper, but didn't know what to do with it. It was as if I momentarily forgot what a pen was for." Russell paused. "Do you think I am still jumping to conclusions?"

"You didn't answer my question. What does McCormick say?"

"That's exactly what I've been talking about," Russell barked. "Your question slipped my mind. All McCormick does is continue to assure me that I am simply rundown and a vacation would cure me."

"Perhaps he is right," Anderson replied, reaching into his medical satchel. "Let me go over you and see what I come up with."

During the following forty minutes Anderson did his best to look undisturbed, but as each positive finding was uncovered, it became more and more difficult to hide his concern. True, there was nothing definitely abnormal, nothing specific that emerged from the physical, but there were suggestions that pointed toward trouble. A hint of an unsteady gait, an indication that Russell had lost a moderate degree of sensation in his right arm and that he had some difficulty in grasping the meaning of abstract statements. True, they were only soft neurological signs, but they were signs nonetheless. However, what disturbed Anderson more than anything was Russell's self-professed memory loss.

Anderson shoved his equipment back into his medical bag, zipped it shut, and turned to his friend. "Everything seems to be in order. I'll confer with McCormick and get back to you. I don't believe there's anything seriously wrong, but I do believe we should run some tests to determine what is causing your symptoms and then start whatever medication is indicated to get you back on your feet again." Anderson swallowed hard, hoping he had sounded convincing. He knew what had to be done. Arrange for the necessary medical tests as quickly as possible and do so without unduly alarming his patient. He could afford to be worried. Russell could not. Russell had too much to accomplish to allow anxiety to interfere with his work.

Dusk lingered. The orange sun inflamed the city's skyline, its rays filtered through the window, spread across the room and bounced off the white ceiling. The hotel had seen better days, but there was a pretense to forgotten elegance that gave the room timelessness, a tranquillity that Anderson needed.

He lay still on top of the pastel bedsheets waiting for McCormick to return his call, feeling spent, washed out. The day had not turned out as originally planned. By now his nightmare was to have ended. Instead he found himself enmeshed in someone else's.

The gnawing emptiness in his stomach was returning. He was angry at Russell for forcing him to live. He had to put a stop to these self-indulgent thoughts. He remembered *The Old Man and the Sea*. Don't think. Just endure. He'd decided to take Hemingway's recommendation when the beige phone beside the bed rang.

"Mike Anderson?" The voice was distant.

"Yes."

"It's Art McCormick. Just got your message. What can I do for you?"

Anderson inhaled deeply. "Russell asked me to fly down today so I could examine him. He was quite insistent. Frankly, I'm disturbed at my findings. I'd like to meet with you immediately."

"I'd like nothing better, but I'm afraid it's impossible. I'm leaving for my weekend place in the mountains as soon as I finish up here," McCormick replied politely, "but I'm glad you called. I've been meaning to get in touch with you for the past few weeks. I'm well aware of the difficulties Russell has been having and am in the process of having tests done. I should have some of the results back in a few days."

"I have known Russell for over thirty years and I've never seen or heard him like this. He is scared, and I think he may well have reason to be," Anderson said, his voice rising. "We've got to find out why he is collapsing mentally and physically."

"Hold on, I told you I should have some answers by midweek," countered McCormick.

"Okay, okay, but we can't afford to waste time. I know he

is your patient and that he is my best friend, but more important than that, he is the president of the United States."

Sweat poured in rivulets down from the receding gray hairline and down both sides of the doctor's stubby, pugnacious nose. Dark circles had formed under his armpits. Even the front of the man's shirt was damp.

McCormick rubbed his eyes and wiped the beads of sweat from his forehead. He looked at his watch, tapped his index finger nervously on the desk, and then abruptly sprang to his feet. He mixed himself a double martini and gazed out the window. The spill from the streetlights cast shadows on the nearby Potomac.

Tension began to envelop him. He fumbled for a cigarette, lit it, inhaled deeply, poured another double martini and reached for the phone.

"Listen, I've got to cancel our weekend plans. I hope you will understand but something important has come up. One of my patients has just had a heart attack, and I'd better stick around. I promise I'll make it up to you."

The doctor's fear lessened as the voice on the other end of the line calmly accepted the unexpected change in plans. He sighed in relief. Now he had time to consider what needed to be done to restore control over the situation.

Two

COULD HE PULL HIMSELF TOGETHER LONG ENOUGH TO help Russell? While he was in Washington, he had been able to contain his doubt, but since returning to his Manhattan duplex three hours ago his uncertainty surfaced. Outside the rain had stopped, and the sun was breaking through the heavy cloud cover. It promised to be another sweltering early August afternoon. The city was quiet. The steps at the Metropolitan Museum across the street from his apartment, frequently knee-deep in people, were now deserted. Anderson knew what he had to do. Clear up his calendar and return to Washington. The sooner the better. Yet by staring at the stillness outside his window he was deliberately causing himself to feel lonely and isolated. He never understood why he took pleasure in doing this, but he knew he did. He poured several ounces of Jack Daniels into a tumbler, added ice cubes, and quickly swallowed a large mouthful. His best friend, the most powerful man in the free world, was depending on him. Although worrying about Russell and not believing Art McCormick was as concerned as he ought to be, Anderson nevertheless was allowing self-pity to overtake him. He walked slowly into his bedroom, the ice in his glass crackling as it melted. He took another sip of bourbon. The alcohol was working its special magic, transporting Anderson back to another time, another place, a happier time. The Second World War had ended. Peace was in the air and the optimism of youth had yet to fade.

Those years were filled with just the right blend of hard work and gaiety. The only disturbing rumble: women. He didn't understand why, but he and women didn't mix well. First came the disaster with Ruth Gibson, the librarian at Yale, followed by the fiasco with Eileen Gordon on Cape Cod.

After those experiences Anderson made a conscious decision to foresake closeness and the pain that seemed inevitably to accompany intimacy. He was too vulnerable to cope with these intense feelings. From then on, he would have casual relationships. Once he felt himself starting to care, he'd abruptly stop seeing that woman and go on to another.

He began to plow into his studies, then into his internship, residency, and finally into his private practice. Initially the effort was deliberate but gradually his patients became his lifeline. He cared for them. They cared for and respected him. In time his reputation grew; so did his clientele. Housewives gave way to middle management executives, and they in turn to foreign and domestic dignitaries with a smattering of Hollywood celebrities to complete the package.

Anderson's friendship with John Russell was the one ongoing relationship he maintained. And the fabric was woven in large part by his being Russell's internist.

Anderson had fully expected he'd slip into old age without altering his life-style. Then came the past few years and the unrelenting pain.

The effects of the alcohol were lessening. Anderson slowly moved away from the mirror, kicked off his loafers, and, pushing the deep blue down quilt aside, lowered his long frame onto the bed.

He knew he had to stop these incessant ruminations. Such self-indulgences, no matter how justified, had to wait, at least until he had diagnosed and treated Russell. His findings yesterday had pointed to a real possibility that something was seriously wrong with the way the president's brain was functioning.

He glanced at his gold Rolex watch—three-forty-five. Russell, a man of routine, would be swimming in the White House pool. It was the perfect time to call Peg, to question her about her husband's condition. He was very fond of Peg. She was one woman he felt comfortable with. Warm, sensitive but stable, reliable, trustworthy. As he reached for the phone to dial her private number, he recalled the only time he had seen her ill at ease.

It was the eve of the Inauguration. John was ebullient, bubbling, excited. Peg's brown eyes looked strained, her facial muscles tense.

Although a graduate of the Wharton School of Business and for many years an executive at IBM, she gave up her career when she married John. He was already an ambitious congressman from Richmond, Virginia. She had witnessed enough marital casualties in the political arena to know their marriage could only survive if she devoted a great deal of time and energy to it. Splitting herself between her husband and her own high-pressure career would lead to a double disaster. She weighed her priorities and made her decision. Her one regret was that they were unable to have any children.

On that evening she was filled with doubt, fearful of assuming the responsibilities expected of a first lady. Russell walked over to her, put his arms gently around her waist and began allaying her worry by recounting stories about past first ladies, how they had all emerged as persons in their own right, women who became loved and respected by the people. When he had finished, Peg's face had softened, and she smiled.

Russell, as usual, was right. Peg wore her new role as if it were custom-tailored for her. And the American public appreciated her painstaking efforts to beautify urban America.

Anderson waited as the phone kept ringing.

"Hello, Mrs. Russell's office," a soft-spoken female voice answered. "Who is it?"

"Martha, is that you?" Anderson believed he recognized the voice. He had met Martha Jordan, Peg's private secretary, several times over the past three years.

"Yes, it is. Who is this please?"

"It's Anderson, Mike Anderson. What are you doing picking up Peg's private line? I thought this was Sunday. Don't tell me she has you working seven days a week."

"Oh, hello, Dr. Anderson. Sorry I didn't recognize your voice. Mrs. Russell asked me to finish writing a speech she is to deliver this Wednesday to a group of urban planners in Atlanta."

"Can I speak to her?"

"She's not here."

Anderson tried to hide his surprise. "What is she doing, swimming with the president?"

Jordan laughed. "I've always gotten a kick out of your sense of humor. But I'm serious, she's not in town. She is in Toronto with Mr. Carlotti."

"Who's Carlotti?"

"Don't tell me you've never heard of Antonio Carlotti, the famous clothes designer," Miss Jordan replied in disbelief. "Mrs. Russell flies to Toronto at least three times a year to have him outfit her."

Anderson was confused by Peg's behavior. She was an observant person. How could she be in Canada on a shopping trip while John was ill? Was it possible that she was unaware of her husband's memory lapses and other recent difficulties? Walking into the living room to refill his glass, he realized he'd never understand women.

Three

CAFFEINE ALWAYS SHARPENED ANDERSON'S MIND FOLlowing sleepless nights. Last night's sleep had been frequently interrupted by rehashing his conversation with Martha Jordan. Now he poured fresh coffee into a porcelain cup, marked with narrow blue and gold bands, a housewarming gift from Kate Robins when he moved into the apartment last year.

The coffee was strong and savory. Anderson took another swallow before setting the cup down on the white Formica kitchen table next to the copy of *The New York Times*. The highlight of living in the Big Apple, he mused, unlocking the front door and finding the *Times* waiting to be scooped up. He took another sip of coffee, flipped the paper over and glanced at a headline:

RUSSELL REVERSES POSITION

Anderson, intrigued, read on.

> In an apparent about-face, President John Russell agreed yesterday not to veto the bill passed by both houses of Congress making abortions illegal. The President has come out of hiding with a bang. After two months of hibernation, Russell has reappeared in the news

and captured center stage by renouncing a campaign pledge. What effect this reversal of position on such an emotionally loaded issue will have on his credibility and hence his reelection bid remains to be seen.

Anderson was startled. Over the years Russell and he debated many matters. There wasn't an issue on which the president's views were clearer or more vocal than abortion. Was it possible for a connection to exist between his sudden about-face on this issue and the recent memory loss and physical changes he was undergoing? Anderson believed something was wrong, very wrong, and only after finishing diagnostic tests would he know for certain what it was.

He glanced at the battery-operated brown porcelain clock above the sink. Ten-thirty. Russell's morning briefing would be over and his first appointment for the day still several minutes off. The perfect time to call him and arrange for the work-up. He called on a line only Russell and Ragland had access to. The fewer people involved in what was going on the better. No reason to encourage potentially destructive gossip.

A woman's soft voice answered. Anderson recognized it as belonging to Peg Russell.

But how was that possible? Yesterday, Martha Jordan had told him that Peg was in Toronto and he had taken it for granted that she would still be out of town this morning.

"You caught me off guard, I expected John or Brent to answer this line," Mike said, deciding to act nonchalant rather than surprised.

"Their meeting ended earlier than usual, and they just left. You'll have to settle for me. I didn't know you called John on this number."

"I usually don't, but I wanted this conversation to be private." Anderson laughed weakly. "You know where John went?"

"I believe he and Brent were going for a walk out in the gardens. They should be back in a short while. May I ask what is so important?"

Anderson was bewildered. Peg seemed oblivious to what was going on around her. "I'm worried about John. I called yesterday to speak with you. Martha told me you were out of town."

"That's funny. I thought she knew I canceled the trip," Peg replied.

"You mean you were at the White House all weekend?" Anderson asked, trying not to sound startled.

"Except for a few hours on Saturday when I had a luncheon at the Mayflower. Why these questions?"

Anderson realized he had to pull back. "I'm sorry. I didn't mean to pry. As I said, I'm worried about John."

"In what way!"

"The way he's been acting."

"What do you mean? You haven't seen us for over a month."

It was becoming harder for Anderson to remain calm. "I've had a few chats with him on the telephone. He doesn't sound like the old John," he replied. A white lie at this time appeared the wisest course of action.

"The strain of the presidency is catching up with him. He's tired, that's all. McCormick suggested he take a two-week break, but you know John," Peg answered. She quickly changed the subject. "How about flying down to dinner sometime this week? That way we can get to see one another, and you will see for yourself that John's fine."

Anderson paused before replying. His mind felt like a computer gone haywire. The input was contradictory. The more questions he asked, the less clear things became. He needed to accept Peg's explanation about the weekend or he wouldn't be able to concentrate on the really important task: to diagnose and then treat the president. "I'd love to," he replied.

"How's tomorrow?" Peg asked matter-of-factly.

"That's fine. I'll see you tomorrow evening at about six."

Five minutes after replacing the phone in its cradle, he realized another important matter had been sidestepped. Why hadn't Russell told Peg that Anderson had examined him Saturday at the White House?

Anderson shrugged his shoulders and looked at his watch. That was between them. He wasn't about to get involved in their affairs. He had enough trouble with his own. Tomorrow evening he'd start Russell's work-up. It was eleven o'clock. If he didn't get a move on, he'd be late for hospital rounds, afternoon office hours, and this evening's dinner with Kate.

Kate Robins was becoming impatient. She had hurried her last client to ensure punctuality. That was an hour ago.

She ordered another sidecar and glanced around Le Madrigal, the restaurant Michael suggested because of its excellent French cuisine. The restaurant had the appearance of being frozen in time. Once lovers flirted and courted here. The most famous were long divorced, but the citrus-striped room with its small garden still looked fresh.

Kate caught herself staring at the couple at the next table. She in white face and knickers, he in hard rock attire, a duo especially striking among the tweed, flannel, and black creperie indigenous to this zip code.

Kate, tall, thin, with long ebony hair, high cheekbones, and a full sensuous mouth, was by all standards a stunning woman. Of late she had obtained recognition, long sought, in a field dominated by Chippendale and Hepplewhite of the past and Eames and Bertoia in the present. The Robins chair was being heralded as one of the most innovative pieces of furniture design in years. Knoll was displaying the chair prominently in their showroom.

But she had paid dearly for devoting so much of her time and energy to her career, for not being willing to compromise with her ambition. Past thirty, never married, she dreaded the future. To age alone, without someone to grow old with, terrified her. Then came the ski weekend in Sun Valley and Michael.

She sensed in Anderson, from the onset, a certain hesitancy, a reluctance to get involved. She was as much attracted by his appearance as by the challenge he presented. And over the three years, there had been progress. Not perfection, but progress. Their life together was often an emotional roller coaster. She'd press him, he'd back off. They'd quarrel, not speak for a week or two, and then one or the other would call and initiate a truce. As each crisis arose, was dealt with, and passed, Kate felt their caring grow. But, of late she believed she was not reaching him. That he was pulling away. There was an impatience in his voice, an irritation that was new. The tone and cadence of his words had taken on an eerie, detached quality, setting off a rising level of dissatisfaction within her. Perhaps she was wasting her time. She deserved better.

Anderson's voice interrupted her thoughts. "Kate, forgive me. I was busy doing some paperwork at the office and forgot the time."

That did it. She had to confront him to regain her self-respect. She tolerated playing second fiddle to his patients, even to his fears, but to paperwork, never.

"Sit down. I want to talk to you," she said coldly.

Anderson took a seat alongside Kate and turned towards her. "Must we talk now? I've got too much on my mind. I'd like to have a quiet pleasant evening," Anderson replied, oblivious to the chilliness in her voice.

"That's the way it always is. You decide on everything. What we'll do. Where we'll go. When we'll see each other. Even when we'll talk about it. I'm about fed up."

"Keep your voice down. What the hell is bugging you?" His eyes darted around the crowded room.

"We've been seeing each other for three years. Three years, Michael! If you're not aware of it that's a long time."

"So!" Anderson was rapidly becoming tense. The pain was returning.

"I'm beginning to feel used. Tell me if sex is all you want from our relationship, because if that's the case, I want out."

"Don't be ridiculous, Kate. Calm down." Anderson quickly downed his martini and ordered another.

"Just what do you want?" Kate demanded.

"Why can't things stay as they are?"

Her hands began shaking. "Because I want more. I'm thirty-three. I want children, a home, the works. I had hoped with you, but if that's not the way it's meant to be, I'd better face it now." Kate threw her napkin down, pushed herself from the table, briskly turned, and walked away.

Anderson stared at Kate as she stormed out of the restaurant, the tension in his body lessening. The pain was gone.

A barrel-chested middle-aged man in a gray herringbone suit seated at a corner table watched Kate's quick exit. When he was certain he wasn't being observed, he slid past the pastry tray, eyeing the chocolate mousse and the fresh strawberries, and walked towards the rear of the restaurant, stopped, placed several coins into the pay phone and squinting in the dim light began dialing.

"The girl's just left," the caller began in his thin Irish accent.

"And Anderson?"

"He's still sitting at the table."

"Good. Keep on his tail and continue to report in. And Brian, remember, nothing physical. I don't want him harmed." The husky voice at the other end of the line paused before continuing. "At least not yet."

Four

BRENT RAGLAND GLANCED AT THE TALL CASE CLOCK made by John and Thomas Seymour of Boston. Set in the corner of the Oval Office, it had kept perfect time for the past two hundred years. He yawned wearily. Ten-thirty P.M. It had been a long and wearing day. It was still too soon to assess the damage caused by today's development. He had spent most of his waking hours dealing with the aftermath of the morning's news story, quieting several members of the Senate and various congressmen who thought they had finally found an issue to nail Russell with, fending off radio, television, and news reporters itching for another coup. For the past two months Ragland had been relatively successful at keeping Russell from the media. He never knew he could be so adept at keeping so many at bay. But after today's events, he was running out of time.

At first Ragland went along with McCormick's opinion. Russell had the flu, nothing more. But as the days stretched into weeks and the president's command of himself continued to diminish, Ragland could no longer accept the doctor's findings. Last Saturday, he had pleaded with Russell to call in Anderson.

Now he feared it was too late. By the time Anderson came up with the answers, all would be academic.

He turned towards Russell, seated on one of the four peach-colored upholstered chairs resting next to a mahogany card table on which stood Frederic Remington's bronze figure of "Bronco Buster." The statue symbolized the vitality, enthusiasm, and boundless energy that the American people had come to associate with their president.

"I'm bushed. How about calling it a night?" Ragland said.

"In about an hour. I must get tomorrow's speech down pat."

"What speech?" Ragland looked surprised. "You don't have any public appearances scheduled for tomorrow."

"That's not true. I promised Lucas I'd address some businessmen from his home town. They'll be in Washington for a few days. He owes them a favor, and we owe Lucas more than that. Don't forget, if it wasn't for his help during the campaign, I doubt if we'd be here now."

Ragland's voice rose. "And after today's disaster, we might not be here for long, especially if you insist on publicly embarrassing yourself."

"Jackson promised he'd keep yesterday's conversation private."

"You've always told me that Jackson couldn't be trusted," Ragland replied. "When you confided to me that your judgment was slipping and asked me to be your go-between I agreed, but if you go ahead anyway and make these plans, how can I protect you?"

"Brent, please. Try and appreciate the spot I'm in. I came on board promising an open administration. To be the people's president. Not to hide behind these walls as recent presidents have. That's what we sold. That's what the voters bought, Brent." Russell paused, his voice strained. "You can't do this to me. I can't go back on my campaign pledge."

"John, you don't know how malleable you've become, how much your judgment and ability to reason have been altered."

Russell's tone suddenly became alive. "Are you suggesting I am no longer fit for office?"

"Of course not. Only that you continue to stay behind the scenes. When it's necessary, either I'll represent you or I'll get Peg to stand in." Ragland halted. To say more would be cruel and unnecessary. "Do I have your word? No further appearances or interviews until Anderson figures out what is the matter. Is that a deal?"

Without replying, Russell walked across the room, opened the door to the hallway, turned back, gave Ragland a somber glare, and left.

Ragland stood speechless, staring at the empty doorway. Seven weeks. That's all that it had been since Russell delivered the talk in Palm Beach. The speech that made it clear that his friend was slipping. Seven weeks. It seemed like years.

Ragland remembered McCormick's attempts to get Russell to postpone his trip to Palm Beach. To rest and allow whatever bug was festering to run its course. However, Russell ignored McCormick's advice, justifying his stubborness on the grounds that the two-hundred-dollar-a-plate dinner would guarantee to be a sellout only if he appeared. The proceeds were badly needed and would put a large dent in the Republican Party's debt.

The Breakers was overflowing. Halfway through Russell's speech on tax reform, a skirmish broke out in the kitchen. Nothing serious. The authorities restored peace but Russell, distracted, was never able to regain his composure. He stumbled over words, jumbled sentences, left out entire paragraphs.

Since Florida, Ragland had kept a tight rein on the president. The mistakes Ragland feared never materialized.

Then came today.

He shuddered, checked his watch: eleven o'clock. He would try Anderson once more before retiring.

The phone was picked up after the third ring.

"Mike, it's Brent. I've been trying to get you all night."

Anderson swallowed hard. "What's wrong?"

"Peg told me you're coming over tomorrow evening for dinner. I'd appreciate it if you could cancel whatever appointments you've made and come earlier. I didn't get a chance to be alone with you after you saw John. There are certain things I need to fill you in on. I don't believe his memory is sharp enough to have given you an accurate account of what's been happening to him."

"You sound more concerned than when we spoke on Saturday."

"I am. You saw today's paper, didn't you?"

"I did," Anderson gloomily replied. "I'll fly down first thing in the morning and Brent, register me at the Quality Inn, Capitol Hill, in case I need to stay over."

Five

RUSSELL GUIDED ANDERSON FROM THE DINING ROOM into the sitting room, and across an Iranian Tabriz rug to a green plush chair beside a table that held a bottle of Johnny Walker, some glasses on a tray, and a box of cigars. Twilight was dimming the room. He stood there in the weakening light, lit a cigar, poured each of them a drink, and slumped down on a nearby couch.

"You know I always wanted you to come on board, both as my doctor and my friend. After the election, I envisioned Ragland, you, and I together again. Much as it was at Yale, only on a grander and more important scale. Perhaps my motives were selfish. I always envied you your memory. Your ability to read so rapidly and spit the material out verbatim would have been a godsend in this office. I can't tell you how many hours a day I spend plodding through the news, position papers, and detailed memos from countless sources. Things I have to read. Material I must know. And that was when I was sharp. Now—" Russell halted, anxiety coming into his reddened face. His eyes moved jerkily up and down, shifting their focus uneasily between the floor and Anderson's concerned face. "I had no right to demand that of you, so I didn't press it. Now I wish I had. You would have been here when I started feeling sick. It's not that McCormick isn't a good doctor. I'm sure he is. He did a great job last fall when my appendix was about to rupture. It's that I've known you longer than anybody else. Longer than Peg. Whenever I've been in need, you've always been the one I turned to."

"That's why I came when you called, why I'm here now," Anderson said.

"Mike, even though I've shared more with you than with anyone else, I'm sure you know I'm basically a private person. There is something I have to tell you. Something I've never told anyone. I believe it'll explain why I'm so frightened.

"At Yale, those phone calls I'd get in the middle of the night," Russell paused, drawing his brows together.

"What about them?"

"They were from my mother. At those times, she couldn't cope with my father and needed to talk. You remember my father from our earlier years at Yale. When he'd visit and take us out for dinner. We'd drink and laugh. He was fun to be around. But then the visits stopped. You asked, but as I said, I'm a private person. I never told you why."

Anderson leaned forward in his seat and poured another drink.

Russell continued. "It began when I called home one day and my father abruptly hung up the phone. On our Christmas break, he seemed obsessed with the plumbing. He would look under the sink, start to take apart the pipes, convinced there was a leak. He would walk away in the middle of conversations. He repeated himself. He looked depressed. When I came home for spring recess, he was quiet, withdrawn, and sometimes would look at Mother and me and say, 'What's wrong with me?' Dad was a damned good trial lawyer. Then suddenly, Mother began hearing from his colleagues how he was not himself. He'd come to court ill-prepared. Oftentimes late. Occasionally disheveled. He'd lose track of his argument, forget pertinent facts during cross-examinations, and embarrass himself during summation. In our senior year, he was asked to resign," Russell's voice cracked.

"What did his doctor say?" Anderson asked.

Anguish clouded the president's eyes. "Initially, he was told he had the flu." Russell glanced at his friend. "Sound familiar?" He poured another drink and continued, "Then they thought he was suffering from depression. But none of the medication helped. He was past the point of misplacing keys. He would forget we had a burglar alarm and would set it off regularly. One night he woke Mother with a fistful of colored, mangled wires. He had set off the alarm, and not knowing how to shut it off, had ripped the wires from their connection in the control box." The pain on Russell's face was evident.

Russell glanced at Anderson. "A few days before you and I were to leave for the summer, our junior year over, the two of us were at Morley's downing a few drafts when Ragland barged in. He said my mother called and sounded frantic. Father had killed our two Labrador retrievers. He took them to the vet and had them put to sleep. His reason: he was afraid they were going to kill him."

Russell went on. "I had Mother make an appointment with a neurologist in town, and I flew home. I couldn't believe what had happened in the three months since I had last seen my father. He didn't know the day of the week. He wasn't clear about the time of the day. He turned to me at the doctor's office, frightened, wanting help.

"By the time I returned for our senior year, Father couldn't be left alone. He'd leave the oven on, get into car accidents. We had to get a live-in companion to spell Mother, or she'd have cracked from the strain. What a senior year. It was a nightmare, but it was mine. I didn't feel it was right to burden you with the sordid details and somehow or other, because you and Ragland didn't know what was happening, it enabled me at times to deny the reality and enjoy myself."

Russell put his glass down on the nearby tray. "Need I continue? I'm sure you've gotten the point. My father was fifty-eight when his memory problems started. I'll be fifty-eight in November. The parallels between his condition and what's been happening to me are too great to throw off as mere coincidence."

Anderson nodded with emphasis, his eyes questioning. "What label did they tack onto his illness?"

"Alzheimer's disease." Russell blurted the words out. "Father died, as you know, during my second year at law school. The last ten months of his life he was a vegetable. He didn't recognize any of us. He spoke nonsense words. His mind was totally shot. I was relieved when he died."

Anderson eyed his friend. "Aren't you jumping the gun a bit?"

"I began reading up on Alzheimer's after I became senator. At the time, I didn't know why my sudden interest in learning about the illness, but I began reading all the articles I could find on the subject. Peg believed I was becoming obsessed and blamed it on my turning fifty. About two years later, I had myself convinced that I was going to follow in my father's footsteps, and by fifty-eight would inevitably be proved right. A month before my symptoms started, I read an article by a Dr. Peter Davies, a neuroscientist at the Albert Einstein College of Medicine, in New York, who believes there is a strong possibility that Alzheimer's is genetic. Lonnie Wollin, the president of the New York chapter of the Alzheimer's Disease and Related Disorders Association, had five family members, his father, his father's two brothers, and two sisters, all of whom are victims. Wollin's family is an example where Alzheimer's shows a strong family pattern, and Dr. Davies believes a gene is involved in these familial cases."

Russell lifted his feet to the couch and stretched out. "Mike, I am a doomed man."

Anderson, still stunned by Russell's revelation, was slow to respond. "I'm not agreeing or disagreeing with you. You've presented a strong case, but as a doctor, I am well aware of more than fifteen other conditions that have identical symptoms to the ones you've developed, and most of those can be treated and cured."

"My grandfather, my father's father, also died of Alzheimer's. Mike," Russell said, "can't you see that's been the reason all my life why I've been so driven? Why I've had to accomplish everything so fast? Yes, of course, I want you to do a thorough work-up, and I'd love nothing more than to be proven wrong. But that's not the most urgent matter. That's not why I finally gave in to Ragland's demand to call you. Regardless of your findings, what I need is your guarantee, your promise, to do whatever is necessary over the next two months so I can function as close to normal as possible. After that, my most important task will be over, and come what may, I'll be at peace with myself, knowing I've accomplished what I set out to do."

"And what is that?"

"I can't tell you. Only a few people know about this matter. But what I will tell you is that I must be able to be alert, have total control of my thoughts, my mind has to be able to think rationally. Rapidly. I must be disciplined and reason perfectly. If not— I don't want to think of what might happen."

The president looked pleadingly at Anderson. "Can you do that?"

Anderson tried to remain detached. To work effectively, he couldn't allow his emotions to influence his clinical judgment. He had to maintain his objectivity. "What tests has McCormick run?"

"None that I know of. No, I take that back. When I first

complained to him, he took a few blood tests and a chest X-ray, but as far as I know, they were normal."

"That's odd," Anderson's voice registered surprise. "I called Art on Saturday, after I examined you, and he told me he had run some tests but hadn't received the results back as yet. I'd better make a note of calling him and finding out what tests he was referring to. And when I speak to him, I'll tell him to set everything up. The evaluation should be done in a hospital."

Russell interrupted. "No, Mike. I have to insist you do all the tests right here in the White House. I have to be assured of absolute secrecy. You'll have to trust me on this. I can't tell you why, but I can't go to a hospital. It's too risky. Sooner or later, the media would find out I'm there, and everything I've worked for would be ruined. No, I'm afraid you'll have to use your ingenuity and figure out what tests you have to do and how you'll do them right here."

"That's some task," Anderson replied.

"That's the way it must be. And one more thing before you go back to the hotel. Don't tell Peg about our talk. As it is, she's quite upset about my illness, and I want to spare her further worry. So please, whatever you find out, tell me. I'm in a better position to know what to tell Peg. She's not as strong as you might think."

Anderson was dazed. He felt like Sonny Liston after being struck by Muhammad Ali's lethal one-two combination. The shock of finding out about Russell's father hadn't been digested. Now Russell was painting a picture of Peg as a distraught wife.

Peg worried? Anderson had a hard time believing that. His dealings with her so far indicated a nonchalance bordering on indifference. Yet the president believed she was shaken by his illness.

Anderson was mystified. Questions, only questions, and so far no answers.

* * *

The crescent moon obscured by billowy clouds left Anderson with a glow from the streetlight as his sole companion as he walked past the Franklin Delano Roosevelt Memorial on his way back to the hotel.

He needed it this way. He had to be alone. To have time to let this evening's conversation with Russell sink in.

Alzheimer's disease. He recalled that Down's syndrome, formerly called mongoloidism, and Alzheimer's disease occur more frequently in the same family than chance would have it. Russell had a second cousin and a great-aunt, both on his father's side of the family, who were born retarded. John had once told him they were mongoloids.

Anderson shuddered. In addition, he knew maternal age was considered a risk factor in Alzheimer's disease, with children born to older mothers having an increased risk of developing this condition as adults. John's mother was almost forty when he was born.

He remembered reading that Alzheimer's was the most common form of senility in people younger than sixty. The onset gradual, the course progressive. He knew the rate of degeneration was variable, depending not only on nerve loss and physical deterioration, but the adequacy of the medical and support systems. Fortunately, Russell would have the best available care. Some patients decline abruptly and then plateau. Others remain stable with only a small decline before the onset of rapid deterioration. Change was gradual in some, but he had seen wide fluctuations in others.

The telltale sign in Alzheimer's, Anderson knew, was cognitive dysfunction, which included deficits in attention, learning, memory, and language skills. The patient is simply unable to speak intelligently or to understand what is being said to him. In addition, there are lapses of memory, impairment of judgment, and an inability to communicate.

Mike was forced to admit John had demonstrated memory loss, and as he thought of the *Times* abortion article, perhaps lapses in judgment as well.

Anderson, a fervent patron of the arts, quickly passed the east wing of the National Gallery without notice. Capitol Hill loomed in the distance.

The list of possible causes for memory loss raced through Anderson's mind. There were the reversible ones: those due to tumors or trauma. There were the infectious disorders, such as pneumonia or hidden abscesses, that could cause this. Then there were a host of metabolic disorders that had to be ruled out. Electrolyte disturbances caused by diuretics was also a possibility. However, John wasn't taking any medications. Thyroid disease, diabetes, calcium irregularities also had to be considered. Other avenues to explore were nutritional problems, circulatory and pulmonary diseases. At least he could dismiss two frequent causes of reversible memory loss in John's case. Alcoholism and psychiatric difficulties.

He hoped his tests would pick up one of the disorders modern medicine was equipped to cure. But reluctantly he forced himself to drag up the irreversible forms of senility, those illnesses where there was no treatment, no hope. They included basically two groups: Alzheimer's disease and individuals who suffered recurrent strokes.

Anderson, while contemplating how to proceed in the morning, threaded his way past the carefully groomed white miniature poodle pulling along a mustachioed master and entered the hotel. He hoped Russell was wrong. Otherwise, within a few years his brain would forget not only what day it was, but how to perform what for most people were automatic functions: how to eat, how to walk—in short, how to live.

Brian Steele sat inside the dirty gunmetal gray Peugeot, parked across the street from the Quality Inn, and peered at the lanky doctor as he passed the frisky white ball of fluff and disappeared into the crowded lobby. What a missed opportunity. He had followed Anderson from the White House through deserted streets. The conditions to strike had been perfect.

Steele fondled the one-and-a-half-pound modified Smith & Wesson M-39 in his muscular right hand. He loved its smooth body, its compactness, its black Teflon finish. No frills or nickel plate. He admired the transparent grip that allowed a visual count of the 9mm cartridges it held. He noticed a stirring in his loins. No woman was capable of arousing him like that.

Dammit. He couldn't stand this assignment. He was not a run-of-the-mill hit man but a professional of the highest order. His actual name was not Steele at all. His former name, the real one, had ceased to be operative the moment he learned that his developing skills were worth money, all tax-free, if he could remain invisible.

Steele was above the fearless triggers from New York's ghettos and the highly regarded mechanics who were free to choose to a degree, who charged exorbitantly, and who did their work with the neatness of a surgeon. Steele was in a class above them all. He was the one you hired to take care of a mechanic who had gotten out of line, a hit man's hit man.

How then had he let himself be talked into this job? To follow, not to kill. He hated the monotony and the effect on his hemorrhoids from all this sitting and waiting. The sum of half a million dollars wasn't enough to explain why he agreed to take on this task. Maybe it was his hatred for the high and the mighty. Yeah, that must have been it. That and his instincts. He had faith in them. They told him to be patient. To follow orders. To wait. That before long, he'd be told to do what he did best, what he liked best—to kill.

Six

McCORMICK STOOD IN FRONT OF EIGHT DISGRUNTLED faces seated around the oblong walnut table. They had been summoned by Vice-President Bart Kingsley to convene promptly at 9:00 A.M. in the small caucus room of the Dirkson Senate Building. The importance of the issue at hand made punctuality essential and annoyance at having to wait for McCormick inevitable. His consistent tardiness amused those within the White House, but the men glaring across the room at the bulky figure found nothing particularly humorous about having to rearrange their important schedules to wait for the good doctor to make his grand entrance.

Russell and his staff allowed McCormick his peccadilloes. They found he more than compensated for it by strong intelligence, a likable personality, sharp analytical skills, and an astonishingly informative mind. He was an early winner in one of the first big money television quiz shows. His topic: American history. The prize money helped to finance his medical studies.

The doctor's gaze took in the high-ceilinged room, its walls decorated with marble pilasters and its windows draped in maroon, before coming to rest at Kingsley's stare.

"Good of you to join us," the vice-president said, his tone

sarcastic. "I believe you know most of the members of the committee. The others you'll get to know as we go on."

McCormick sat down in the empty seat, sandwiched in between Secretary of State Ron Barrett and Cullie Hamilton, the cherubic Senate majority leader from Alabama.

With characteristic exuberant indignation, Hamilton bellowed. "Look here, McCormick, it's mighty inconsiderate to hold us up like that. We got a little problem and want you to help us out."

McCormick squirmed in his straight-back chair. Paul Harvey, the secretary of defense, nodded in agreement, while the attorney general, Hal Feinstein, his thickened body a large mass under the three-piece suit, muttered to Hamilton, "Now's not the time to pontificate, Cullie. We've got to stick together."

Gabe Condon, the Speaker of the House, and Tad Winston, the minority leader, turned to their captain, waiting for Kingsley to take command, to steer this band of bloated egos safely to shore.

The eighth man, Morton Edgars, a stranger to the others, face expressionless, sat at the far corner of the table, stroking his gray beard, observing everything, saying nothing.

Cullie Hamilton chewed the butt of his unlit cigar. "Time is a'wastin'. Let's get the show on the road." Cullie, at seventy, one of a kind, his shell as impenetrable as a Galápagos', knew that like the great turtle he'd soon be extinct. This race against the clock only served to heighten his determination. No one on the Hill could recall his budging on an issue. Once he had a position, regardless of the merits of the opposing argument, he'd stand firm.

This particular senator had undeniable clout. There were lightweight and heavyweight senators. The weak were those who were too new to have established a Washington base, too old to have retained one, or too inept to have built one.

Senatorial power rested in those relatively few members of the upper house who had planned and painstakingly built and ratcheted every grain into a wedge of enduring strength. Such was Cullie Hamilton, who had enough leverage to move a lot of people, including Bart Kingsley.

The vice-president received Hamilton's go-ahead signal and began. "You all know why you were summoned to this meeting. Before we discuss the specific predicament we face, I have asked Dr. McCormick, one of our leading experts in American history, to share his knowledge about President Woodrow Wilson's medical problems, how they were handled, and how they affected our nation's course, so we will be better prepared to prevent history from repeating itself." Kingsley sat back, folding his arms across his chest. "Doctor, the floor is yours."

McCormick opened the file folder. His full face was made more so by a tight shirt collar that pressed into the flesh of his neck. "President Wilson and his wife were touring the country to rally the support of the American people to get the League of Nations ratified. Wilson began developing severe and recurrent headaches that necessitated cutting the trip short and returning to Washington. At eleven on Sunday morning, September 28, 1919, the train pulled into the capital. Once at the White House, the president wandered like a ghost between the study at one end of the hall and his wife's room at the other. The acute pain in his head was too severe to permit work or even reading.

"For the next two days, Wilson rested and seemed a little better. Then shortly after 8 A.M. on the third day after returning home, Mrs. Wilson awoke and found her husband sitting on the side of the bed trying to reach a water bottle. She handed it to him and noticed his left hand hung loosely. She assisted him to the bathroom. He moved with great difficulty and every move brought spasms of pain. Alarmed, she called Dr. Grayson, her husband's physician, and while on the phone heard a noise, rushed into the bathroom, and found him on the bathroom floor unconscious. He had suffered a stroke, paralyzing the left side of his body." McCormick paused, allowing the words to have their desired impact. Feinstein stopped shuffling papers. Barrett put down his half-eaten Danish.

Satisfied, the doctor continued. "Wilson remained incommunicado for several months, while Mrs. Wilson acted as a buffer between the president and the outside world. The doctors informed Mrs. Wilson that recovery couldn't be hoped for unless the president was relieved of every disturbing problem during those days, so nature's efforts to repair the damage done could proceed. This advice, by the way, was exactly what the Russian and German physicians who attended Lenin four years later for his stroke advised, with the same disastrous results to his country.

"Dr. Durcum, one of Wilson's attending physicians, took Mrs. Wilson aside and convinced the first lady that her husband's situation was grave but that she had the ability to cope with it. He told her to have every matter come to her, that she should weigh the importance of each issue, and see if it would be possible by a consultation with the head of the appropriate department to solve them without the guidance of her husband. He played on her sense of responsibility, telling Mrs. Wilson that for her husband to resign would have a bad effect on the country, and a serious effect on his patient, that he had staked his life and made his promise to the world to do all in his power to get the treaty ratified and make the League of Nations complete. If he resigned, his greatest incentive for recovery would be gone.

"Mrs. Wilson followed the doctors' orders and shielded the president from any event or problem that might upset him. His two physicians, Grayson and Durcum, were concerned as friends." McCormick's intense brown eyes focused on Cullie

Hamilton. "You can relax, Russell and I are not friends. Ours is strictly a doctor/patient relationship. But it's important to know what happened because Grayson was a close friend of the president, his companion, and was regarded by Mrs. Wilson as a member of the family.

"On October sixth of that year, the entire Cabinet met to obtain information about the president's condition, similar to what we are in the process of doing. However, Grayson not only refused to declare the president disabled, but also wouldn't tell the Cabinet anything beyond the fact that Wilson was suffering from a nervous breakdown, indigestion, and a depleted condition, adding the warning that any excitement might kill him." McCormick let the message sink in.

"To compound matters, Presidential Secretary Joseph Tumulty declared he wouldn't be a party to ousting a chief who had been so kind, loyal, and wonderful to him, especially when the president was 'lying on the small of his back.' "

Stillness blanketed the room. Kingsley's voice pierced the air. "So you're suggesting Wilson's illness was responsible for what happened to the League of Nations!"

At this, there was a sudden stirring, the committee members restless in their seats. McCormick's voice became, if anything, more emphatic. "I most certainly am stating just that. Wilson's problems didn't start then. He had a stroke thirteen years before while president of Princeton University. His was a case of long-standing progressive cerebral arteriosclerosis with associated brain damage that resulted in his rigid, compulsive personality becoming tremendously exaggerated, so when he suffered that stroke at the height of his battle with the Senate for ratification of the Versailles Treaty, which included approval of the League of Nations, he was at the point where he was unable to compromise and in the process defeated his own baby. I am sure that had he not involved himself in the Senate debate the United States support of the

League of Nations wouldn't have been defeated. To put it simply, his personal characteristics angered so many of his colleagues they lost sight of the wisdom inherent in creating the League as a strong, independent, peacekeeping force." He turned confidently in Cullie Hamilton's direction.

"What in God's name does this lecture on ancient history have to do with Russell's health problem?" the senior senator from Alabama asked.

"If you'd bear with us for once, maybe you'd get the point," Kingsley said icily.

Hamilton glared at the vice-president, leaned back and chewed on the wet cigar stub, his massive stomach rising and falling as though steam were churning beneath it.

Kingsley said, "Dr. McCormick, you've observed the president firsthand for the past two years, so you're in the best position to evaluate his physical condition.

"As you're aware, Russell has entered into secret negotiations with the Russian premier, Molonyn, discussions which are set to culminate in a summit conference. The two men have set the agenda, nuclear disarmament. What frightens us is the two world leaders insist on withholding the time and the place for their meeting. They insist on complete secrecy on these two practical matters, maintaining they'd rather call off the summit, and any possibility of reaching accord on this monumental issue, than risk public disclosure. They both firmly believe if the countries involved, their government officials, and other nations find out about the purpose of the summit, the publicity alone will, as in the past, doom the negotiations before they start. That"—Kingsley sighed deeply, staring at McCormick—"is the predicament we face. Are we courting disaster, or can we trust Russell in so delicate a matter? If you feel the president's current state can't withstand the demands and pressure that will be placed on him, we must know. Then we can decide how to go about removing

Russell from office." The vice-president paused, observing his captive audience. "Either Russell represents us with our blessings, or we have to work out an orderly transition. Gentlemen, I'd be a fool to lie, to deny I wouldn't love being president of the United States, but not under these circumstances. We must put aside our personal ambitions at this time and do what's best for our country." Kingsley once again turned toward McCormick. "It's up to you. Where do we stand?"

The doctor laid aside his papers. "As you know, President Russell has been having memory problems. He also demonstrates impairment in his ability to conceptualize and analyze material presented to him. But fortunately, this defect is quite mild. At least that is the case now."

Hal Feinstein interrupted, "Are you saying Russell is senile?"

"No, I'm not. However, his symptoms do point to a slowly evolving form of senility, but a type that takes months, if not years, to develop fully. Right now, Russell manifests the earliest signs of the disorder. I believe as time passes, and his symptoms intensify, he will have to be removed from office, but it is my medical belief we are months away from that eventuality.

"Our president is a man of great pride and determination. The summit means more to him than any of us can imagine. I believe we can keep him mentally alert so he'll be able to handle himself at the summit in a completely competent manner. After the negotiations are successfully concluded, then confront him with the need to step down. He's not stupid. He knows what's happening to him. With his place in history assured, he'll likely agree."

Kingsley adjusted the wire frames on the bridge of his nose. "Dr. Edgars, what's your opinion?"

"I agree with McCormick's viewpoint wholeheartedly. For the past twenty-five years, I've worked as a psychiatrist and evaluated dozens of patients with Russell's symptoms. Thus far there's no evidence the president's mental state has deteriorated so that he'd be a danger to himself or that he'd do harm to the welfare of our nation."

Cullie Hamilton drew on a fresh Cuban cigar. "McCormick has presented a mighty good argument for Russell's mind slippin' a bit. And before that, the good doctor gave us a charmin' lecture on Mr. Wilson's illness. Seems to me he's satisfied Russell will handle himself with utmost dignity and composure at the summit, so, Kingsley, with all due respect, I don't see what the fuss is all about!"

McCormick stopped the vice-president before he could answer. "Senator Hamilton, if I may reply to your question. I hope I didn't give the impression of being nonchalant about President Russell's condition. I believe he can hold his own against the Russian premier, but that's my medical opinion, it's not by any means the gospel. I'm not infallible. I could be wrong. I used Wilson as an illustration of a world leader whose illness progressed with detrimental consequences to our country because I feel we should pay attention to what that tells us. That's not to say we should be alarmists, but we should be aware of what could happen. Let us not forget President Franklin Delano Roosevelt in his weakened state caused by advanced heart disease. Many historians believe Roosevelt's acceding to many of Stalin's demands at Yalta would never have happened if he was physically and mentally stronger at the time."

Kingsley loosened his paisley tie. "Well put, Art. I couldn't have said it better myself. Have you ever considered running for office? Judging by your performance today, I'd say you'd make one hell of a politician."

The vice-president's facial expression suddenly changed. He put his face in his hands and began a slow, steady rubbing of his forehead before looking up. "We now know where we stand. Unfortunately, Russell won't go back on his promise to

Molonyn. By not knowing when or where the summit will be held, other than that it will take place before the end of the year, we're operating at a serious disadvantage." Glaring at Hamilton, he continued. "The job ahead isn't going to be an easy one. We can't allow personal ambition or party loyalty to come between us. If we band together, don't breathe what has been said here to anyone, and stay abreast of Russell's condition, we should be in a position to prevent another League of Nations debacle, another Yalta fiasco."

Condon, Barrett, Winston, Harvey, and Feinstein nodded in agreement. Cullie Hamilton, partially obscured by white bands of smoke, sat motionless.

Kingsley poured himself a tall glass of ice water and quickly drank its contents. "We'll reconvene each week to reassess the situation. We don't want to screw up the summit and Russell's nuclear disarmament peace program, but we don't want to jeopardize our nation by having an incompetent man at the helm. We can't afford to have the Russian contingent at the negotiating table operating at maximum effectiveness while our president is less than fully alert."

Kingsley crushed out his cigarette, adjusted his glasses so he could look over the steel rims: "You've a problem? Spell it out!"

"What I did was wrong. It goes against everything I believe in. I've never been involved in a con job."

"Keep your voice down," the vice-president said. "You owed me one, and I collected. We're even. It's as simple as that. If it wasn't for my being persistent, Russell would have passed you over. You'd never have become his personal physician, so cut out the moralizing bullshit." Kingsley paused, then continued, "Tell me one thing. How'd you convince Dr. Edgars to go along?"

McCormick straightened his broad-shouldered body. "Unfortunately, that was easy. Psychiatrists love it when symptoms can be attributable to a physical disorder rather than a psychological one. So when I told him of my findings, he latched on to them."

The vice-president smiled. "You must understand that what I insisted you do wasn't wrong. All you did was stretch the truth. If you hadn't been so forceful and direct, the committee members would have been divided, nothing would have been accomplished. This way, the members are satisfied with your diagnosis and relieved enough to allow Russell to bring off the summit as planned. Didn't we both feel having Russell meet with Molonyn was essential?"

McCormick reluctantly was forced to agree. "But to falsify a diagnosis?"

"That's beside the point. He's having memory problems and other symptoms which you admitted were all consistent with someone developing senility. If you hadn't presented things the way you did, the picture would have been confusing and the committee would never have agreed to let Russell proceed."

The doctor shook his head in disbelief. "I've always thought of myself as a good judge of people, but you puzzle me. I can't for the life of me figure out why it's so important for you to make sure the summit goes off as scheduled."

Kingsley returned the doctor's stare, slow anger finally surfacing. "That's not your business, is it? You've played out your part, now please leave. And McCormick, next week be here on time!"

McCormick moved out into the street and approached his car, the hot early August heat from the pavement burning through his soles. He valued being his own boss. Medicine afforded him the opportunity to follow his own drummer. Now he was obeying another, operating totally in the dark;

he had been given no clear reason for the job he was doing, and he was powerless to free himself.

He reached into his pocket, pulled out his keys, unlocked the car door and was about to slide into the driver's seat when an arm grabbed him from behind. He turned and glared at his assailant. "Ragland, what the hell's come over you?"

"Just hold it there," answered Ragland, his voice cold. "There doesn't seem to be any other way of getting your attention. You don't return my calls. You cancel our appointments. Now you're forced to hear me out."

"How did you know where to find me?"

"Your secretary was most obliging. She even told me you'd be driving a green Audi. Please thank her the next time you see her. By the way, you don't have any patients here, so what were you doing in the Senate Building?"

"That's none of your business. I never knew I had to report to you."

"Listen, Doc, I've never liked you either, but that's beside the point. It's time you woke up to the fact Russell is more than my boss. He's a very close friend. Anderson believes his condition is far graver than you're letting on. Unless you begin using your medical ingenuity to figure out what is causing Russell to go downhill, I will do everything in my power to convince the president to replace you."

Seven

It was 11 a.m. and raining in Washington. Angry, diagonal sheets were driven by spasmodic winds, making travel by foot or car hazardous. The chauffeur at the wheel of the black-stretch Abraham, heading down Fourteenth Street toward the East Gate of the White House, slammed on his brakes and swerved to avoid an onrushing van.

"Sorry, sir," he said, his voice directed at the intercom, his eyes on the rearview mirror and the glass partition that separated him from his passenger.

The blue intercom light was on, which meant his voice was being transmitted. Anderson didn't respond. He was deep in thought, planning what had to be done before the day was spent. In the past hour, he had secured the needed equipment: a portable X-ray machine, disposable needles and syringes, and test tubes for blood assay. He cursed Russell's stubborn insistence on having the tests done at the White House. The two diagnostic tests that would have shed the most light on what was going on were now an impossibility. Both the CAT scan which, like a road map, shows the specific location of the trouble spot, and the PET scan, which discloses the physical and chemical changes occurring within the brain, utilized complex machinery, accoutrements housed only in hospitals.

He'd have to hope the equipment he brought would prove sufficient. Russell for his part had carefully arranged the day, clearing his calendar for the "private lunch" he and Anderson were to have and convincing Peg to fly to Atlanta early this morning rather than this afternoon for her keynote address at the opening of the city's much heralded mile-long mall.

"We're here, sir," the driver said as he slowed down, switching off the foglights before coming to a stop.

The door of the limousine opened, and a man in his late thirties appeared, umbrella in hand. "The president's expecting you," he yelled through the sound of the downpour. He slammed the door shut and led Anderson into the White House.

Russell, standing by the window watching the torrents of water forming miniature lakes on the White House lawn, briefly wondered how the fish were biting back home in Lake Anna, near Louisa, Virginia. How he wished he were there now.

"I'm all set. Let's get started." Anderson's voice brought Russell back to the Oval Office, to the bewildering reality facing him.

Silently, the president lowered himself into his leather-backed desk chair, first positioning his head as directed while Anderson took a full series of skull films and then positioning his arm while the doctor drew several vials of blood.

"Who are you going to have read these X-rays?"

"His name's Frank Stanton. You don't know him. He's a colleague of mine and a damned good neuroradiologist."

"Can he be trusted to keep quiet?"

"What's come over you? You've never questioned me before."

"You know Walt Dickinson, Peg's father. He runs the *Washington Post*. Because I've shunned the press lately, he suspects something's up. He sent Eric Dawson over this morning. Ragland tried to get rid of him, but he's a persistent bastard. He threatened to write a piece guaranteed to play havoc with people's fears. He didn't elaborate on what he'd say, but he promised he wouldn't go ahead with his plan if I'd grant him an interview. Ragland limited our talk to five minutes, but I'm afraid during that time I messed up a sentence pretty badly."

"Did he catch it?"

"He didn't let on if he did or not, but I've known Dawson for years. He's cagy like a fox and ambitious as hell. When he sniffs a lead, he doesn't let go. He's still bitter about not being selected for last year's Pulitzer Prize for his series on OPEC's attempts to bribe the heads of our large oil corporations so they'd stop their search for hidden oil reserves. An exposé on the president would put him ahead of the pack for this year's award."

Anderson listened, trying to hide his concern. He was now facing three enemies: one, time; two, Peg's casual if not indifferent attitude to her husband's rapidly worsening state; and three, Dawson, a ruthless investigative reporter, who'd love to break the news to the world that John Russell, president of the United States, was critically ill.

Those were just the known enemies he had to contend with. He wondered as he disconnected the X-ray apparatus if there were others.

Dr. Frank Stanton, Chief of Neuroradiology at New York Hospital, eagerly snapped on the viewing box, the fluorescent glow illuminating the screen.

"Let's have a look at what you've got." His hazel eyes jumped from film to film. "It's a good thing you're not an X-ray technician. The quality of these pictures is terrible." He turned his Modigliani profile in Anderson's direction. "Who's the patient?"

"I'm afraid I can't reveal that."

"A bigwig, huh! I've never seen you looking so tense."

Anderson smiled weakly.

"Okay. I'll drop it. How about some history?"

"Several months of decreased mental acuity and increased forgetfulness."

Stanton returned his gaze to the X-rays, his tall, muscular body made more imposing by his proper Bostonian posture.

"Any apraxia?"

Apraxia is the inability to perform certain complex movements, such as knotting a tie, in the absence of paralysis or coordination problems.

"I didn't notice any, but he insists there are times he wants to write but can't do it."

"How about aphasia?"

Aphasia is an impairment in understanding the meaning of the spoken and written word and the inability to express thoughts through speech or writing.

"I tend to think so. During our talks he'd use words that were not in line with the rest of what he was saying."

"And agnosia?"

Agnosia is the failure to recognize common objects.

"Yes. I handed him the thermometer lying on his desk. He turned it in all directions and then stared blankly at me."

"What about the physical exam?"

"Nothing definite. Perhaps a suggestion of right-sided weakness."

"Any eye findings?"

"Equivocal. The optic disks were not engorged, so fortunately there's no indication of increased pressure within the brain."

Stanton raised his index finger to one of the X-rays and with a pencil circumscribed a small white area. "I wouldn't put my reputation on the line, the picture is not clear enough for that, but I believe I'm pointing at the pineal gland. As you know, normally it's located in the dead center, in the middle of the brain. Here it's shifted to the right side. After hearing your description of the history and physical, and looking at these films, I'd lean toward your patient having a mass on the left side of his brain pushing the pineal gland to the right side."

Anderson was stunned. Although he had believed Russell was in trouble, he'd never contemplated this eventuality. "You're saying he has a brain tumor!"

Stanton sat on the edge of his desk. "Don't put words in my mouth. I never said that. I said the odds are he has a space-occupying lesion. I can't even be certain about that. I need better films." His voice took on a sense of urgency. "We need a diagnosis. Whoever this VIP patient of yours is, he is a very, very sick man. I need to see a CAT scan. He must be hospitalized immediately. Until then, all we're doing is speculating and wasting time."

Anderson remained speechless. Stanton glared at him. "I've never seen you like this. You look like a scared, naïve patient rather than an experienced physician who's been in this field for over twenty years. Mike, you'd better shape up. Valuable time is being lost. Time your patient doesn't have. Every minute wasted before a definitive diagnosis is reached drastically decreases your patient's chances for survival."

Anderson bolted from the hospital's marble lobby through the opened door and on the corner of Sixty-ninth Street and First Avenue halted to flag a cab. He lifted his wrist and looked at his watch. It was five forty-seven. He didn't have much time to get to his office and phone McCormick before the doctor left for the day. Now that he had documented proof, McCormick would move swiftly, hospitalize Russell, run the necessary tests, and start treatment. But first he had to get to McCormick. Russell's insistence on secrecy made that difficult. Normally, he'd have called from Stanton's office and the wheels would be in motion.

Several taxis whizzed by. Rush hour. It could be a half hour before one stopped. He couldn't afford to wait. The light was green. He crossed First Avenue and headed uptown past apartment houses, boutiques, and Vietnamese stands with their glistening vegetables and fruit. The rain, driven by wind gusts, pelted against his face. He collided violently with two startled women and a dog-walker, pushing all three forcibly out of the way. He picked up speed, crossed Seventy-second Street and Third against the light, dodging traffic. All actions directed at getting to his office at Seventy-fifth and Park Avenue. People, cars, lights, obstacles in his path. He had to run faster, past the peddlers of capsules and pills, white powder and syringes. He envisioned the rapidly expanding ball of cells inside Russell's brain reaching in all directions like the tentacles of an octopus, killing all life in its way.

Anderson reached Park. Three more blocks. He gasped for air. Sweat pouring down his neck, his legs in agony, his heart exploding inside his chest. All this time, Russell had been fearful of repeating his father's fate, of slowly wasting away until he'd be a vegetable. How would he take the news he was wrong, that he didn't have Alzheimer's disease, but that his end would come in a far more painful way.

He looked up, his office in view. A few more yards and he'd be there. Marathon runners must be crazy, he thought, to enjoy pounding pain.

Anderson raced past the wide-eyed doorman and dashed to the elevator. It was on the nineteenth floor. He glanced at his watch. Six-thirteen. He couldn't wait for it to descend. Taking a deep breath, he sprinted to the stairwell and panted six flights to his office.

He took his key from his pocket and opened the door, turned on the overhead light, reached for the phone and dialed McCormick's number. Be there, McCormick. Please be there, Anderson pleaded as the phone rang.

"Dr. McCormick's office," a perky voice finally responded.

"I'd like to speak to the doctor."

"He's not in. If you'll give me your name and number, he'll call you when he returns."

"I'm Dr. Anderson. I must get in touch with Dr. McCormick immediately. It's about one of his patients."

"Oh, I'm sorry," the receptionist replied apologetically. "I didn't know you were a doctor. He'll be out of town for the rest of the week."

Anderson swallowed hard in disbelief. Perhaps Russell was right in thinking McCormick wasn't taking his illness seriously. "Where is he?"

"He's attending the annual heart meeting in New York City."

"Do you know where he's staying?"

"The Plaza Hotel."

Anderson sighed in relief. He expected he'd have to fly to Washington to show McCormick the X-rays. This simplified matters considerably. Maybe it was an omen that the tide was turning. God, he hoped so. Russell needed all the luck he could get if he was going to survive.

Mike picked up the receiver and dialed the Plaza Hotel. "Dr. Art McCormick's room, please."

Two minutes passed. Finally the switchboard operator returned to the line. "It's busy. Do you wish to hold?"

"Yes," Anderson said. He felt relieved knowing McCormick would be orchestrating the crucial work-up at Walter

Reed Hospital, with its vast medical equipment and team of experts at his disposal.

"The line's still busy. Do you want to hold?"

Anderson thought for a moment. He was wasting valuable time. McCormick was in his room. It would be more efficient to go to the hotel and meet Art directly. "No, that's all right. Thanks anyway."

Five minutes later, Anderson was back on the street heading downtown. He hailed a taxi and slumped into the back seat. He had to calm himself. As long as he was emotionally involved, he wouldn't be in a position to help Russell. There were still not enough medical facts to go on.

As the taxi pulled up to the hotel's majestic Fifth Avenue entrance, Anderson felt the tension in his muscles lessen. He was relieved McCormick would soon be involved, that he wouldn't be in this alone.

Eight

Climbing the steps of the Plaza, it seemed as if he were fourteen again. His mother's voice booming in the distance. He had walked ahead, hypnotized by the grandeur of the hotel. Father was taking them to the Palm Court for Sunday brunch. Anderson had waited anxiously for today, going to sleep for the past several nights hoping the occasion would bring his parents closer together, that his mother would take the gesture as proof his father was changing, that he'd stop drinking, keep a steady job. Maybe then the constant bickering would stop.

During the ride from Connecticut, Anderson's imagined script had changed course. They hadn't been on the Merritt Parkway for more than ten minutes when his mother's nagging started. She berated his father for being a bad provider, using their eight-year-old car and her outmoded dress as evidence, blaming herself for not listening to her parents' objections when she'd announced her engagement. If only she wasn't so stubborn she'd have followed her sister's lead and be living happily in the lap of luxury. No wonder his father drank himself to oblivion, Anderson thought, there was no way to please that woman.

They entered the vast lobby. The sudden sharp snap of flesh on flesh. Father walked away. The dream shattered.

Father and son had visited together while Anderson was at Exeter and later during the years spent at Yale. But the times were fleeting and far between, the closeness they shared irretrievably lost. His mother became a constant reminder of his loss, and her voice the bane of his existence.

How he wanted to sever the cord, but she'd lured him with the promise of a car when he turned seventeen. He swallowed his pride, took her abuse, and waited for the day to come. He sustained himself with the image of taking the keys, turning on the ignition, pressing on the accelerator, and zooming away. He'd be free, never again to have contact with her. Then came the eagerly awaited birthday; a watch. How could she have been so cruel? Rage, hurt, despair, and the beginnings of the stabbing pain in his stomach.

Grim thoughts for a bright, talk-filled lobby. Michael forced them to the back of his mind, and walked towards the bank of telephones, his feet sinking into the thick carpets.

"Dr. Art McCormick's room, please."

"One moment. I'll ring it for you."

"What's his room number?"

"Sorry, sir," the operator replied. "We're not allowed to give that information."

"How about his phone number?"

"Sorry, sir. Same story. Hold on, your party's on the line."

"Art, it's Mike Anderson."

"Anderson! How'd you find me?"

"It's a long story. I'll tell you later. Listen, I have Russell's skull films with me."

McCormick's voice registered surprise. "I wasn't aware you had X-rays taken."

"I was with Russell earlier today and took them myself."

"Where are you?"

"In the hotel. Down in the lobby. I'll come right up. You've got to see them."

McCormick hesitated a moment. "No, I'll be right down. I don't know about you, but I could use a drink. I'll meet you in the Oak Bar."

"Sounds good to me. I'll get us a table by a window. There's still sufficient daylight so you'll be able to read the X-rays."

Anderson, seated at a corner table overlooking Central Park, biting on cashews and sipping Jack Daniels, glanced around the magnificent oak-walled room, the inner trumoil triggered by his past associations with the Plaza gone.

McCormick downed his martini and ordered another. The tall, muscular doctor with determined chin, high-bridged nose, and a broad brow played with the large brass room-key, then slipped it into the pocket of his suit.

Anderson removed an X-ray from the folder and held it against the window, the light shining through, the white area of concern visible, unmistakable.

McCormick gazed at the film with dissatisfaction. "The pineal gland has indeed shifted to the right side of the brain. I feel like a fool, a total ass. I never considered the possibility of a brain tumor. What was the matter with me? Russell kept insisting something was wrong. I kept reassuring him. 'It's the flu, you're rundown. That's all.' "

McCormick was visibly shaken. Anderson's anger towards his colleague started to dissipate. "We'll still have time if we move right away. You've got to convince Russell he must be admitted to Walter Reed immediately."

"That shouldn't be difficult."

Anderson glanced skeptically at McCormick. "Whenever I've broached the subject, he's refused."

"You didn't have positive X-ray findings and besides, by not being his friend, I'm at an advantage. I don't have to worry about his feelings. I'm in a position to do what's medically best. I'll insist he goes in." McCormick gazed at his watch. "It's getting late. I want to call Russell and then make the necessary arrangements. I work with a top-notch neurologist at Walter Reed. I'll have him take charge until I get back to Washington. Unfortunately, I'm presenting a paper at the convention on Friday and have some other matters to clear up, so I'll be in the city until Sunday."

McCormick gulped the rest of his martini. "Let me have the X-rays. I'll have a messenger deliver them to the hospital. That way we'll save time."

"I prefer to keep them. The radiologists at Walter Reed won't be satisfied with their quality. They're going to repeat them anyway."

"As you wish." McCormick fished for the olive at the bottom of his glass. "I'll get the ball rolling. We know how to reach one another. Let's make sure we touch base. And one more thing, Mike. As I'm sure you realize, we must keep this strictly confidential."

McCormick swallowed the olive and quickly threaded his way through the crowd hovering around the bar. Anderson sighed in relief. He felt more optimistic about Russell's chances now that he and McCormick were going to be working together.

Anderson thought the day would never end. Hospital rounds, teaching conferences, patient after patient. The last one finally gone. His secretary had left for the evening. His mind was focused elsewhere. At Walter Reed. What were they finding? Did Russell have a growth? If so, was it operable? Nagging, gnawing questions. Having to wait for McCormick's call rather than being the one in charge added to his out-of-control feeling.

Suddenly the door to his examining room burst open; a

burly, well-dressed man stood under the glare of the overhead lights.

Anderson's gaze fixed on the stranger. "What can I do for you?"

Instead of answering immediately, the intruder closed the door and reached into his pocket. "I'm not a patient," he replied, an Irish accent noticeable.

Anderson wondered what he was doing. And then it was clear. In his right hand was a modified Smith & Wesson M-39 automatic.

"You're in the wrong place. I don't have any drugs."

The stranger inched closer. "I'm not here for drugs."

"You can have whatever you want. My wallet's in my coat."

The man's temper erupted. "Shut up! I'm not here for drugs or money."

Anderson had to think rapidly, stay calm; be ready for the man's next move. He'd been mugged and robbed in his office and had his car burglarized in the past. He didn't know why, but he sensed something different this time. The man's dress, speech, the way he carried himself, all pointed to some other motivation. "What do you want?" Anderson asked.

"I said, 'Shut up.' " There was a click; the hammer of the gun snapped into firing position.

Anderson swallowed hard. Regardless of the outcome, he'd put up a fight. Not valuing his life made it easy to defend himself. If he was to be killed, so be it; the pain would be over.

He had to act fast. He lunged at the gunman, but not in time. He heard the muted spit and felt a razorlike cut across the skin of his neck. An eruption of blood spread over his shoulder. He spun to the right, a second shot followed, the bullet embedding itself in the wall above him. He swung his arm in a violent arc, sending a lamp off the nearby table, towards the intruder standing three feet away in the center of the room, in his gaze the determination of an experienced killer.

Anderson dove to the floor, his fingers gripping the base of the table, lifting it by its legs like a small battering ram. He rose, crashing forward; another shot was fired, splintering the wood above his head.

He rammed the assassin, hammering him back into the wall with such force that a stream of saliva accompanied the expulsion of breath from his snarling lips.

The gun clattered to the floor. Anderson dropped the table, slamming it down on the killer's feet, kicking the gun out of reach.

The doctor crouched, swung his right arm wildly, furiously at his attacker. He lunged again, his right arm arcing up from the floor smashing into his assailant's groin.

The man grimaced in sudden agony. Anderson held the Irishman upright, and with his blood-soaked left arm jammed his fist into the man's lower rib cage.

His assailant, more stunned and angry than battered, rebounded quickly, leaping on Anderson, clawing at the doctor's face. He wrapped his arm around Anderson's neck, spinning him around, crashing his right knee into his victim's kidney, dragging him backward, down onto the floor.

He scissored Anderson's waist with his legs, forcing his neck into a painful arch. Anderson, immobilized, watched helplessly as his assailant grabbed the automatic lying near the desk. He shut his eyes, waiting for the inevitable.

There was a sudden loud thud. Anderson's body smashed violently against the floor. Then there was silence. He glanced around the office. He was alone. Where was his attacker?

He grabbed on to the chair and lifted himself, sharp bolts of pain searing through his chest.

Why had his killer left him alive?

He reached for the phone on his desk. Automatically, without thought, he began dialing.

"Hello, Kate. Come over right now—please." He let the phone crash against the desk top and drop to the floor.

He heard her through mists of pain. He saw her and what he saw was unreasonable—as unreasonable as the pain. She was kneeling beside him, touching his face, touching his head. *Stop it! Do not touch my head. Leave me.*

"Why did you do that?" It was her voice, not his.

What was she doing? She had found sterile bandages in his medicine chest and was wrapping them around his neck. With her other hand she was gently washing the blood from his face. She had loosened his belt and was pushing soft smooth gauze down into the boiling hot skin on his right hip.

Then he remembered his phone call. He found words and used them quickly. He wanted peace and darkness as he had wanted it before, and he could find it if she left him. But he was the one who had called her to come over.

The rays of the setting sun streamed through the window and mottled the walls with irregular shapes of light. Anderson lay back on the couch exhausted.

Kate sat next to him in a leather armchair, her gaze fixed on his face. "You kept saying it," she said softly, spacing out her next words, " 'I don't know—I wish I knew.' You'd stare at something, and I was frightened. I'd ask you what happened. And you'd say it again, 'I wish I knew.' My God, what you've been through—what you're going through. What in God's name happened?"

Anderson leaned on his side, wincing in pain. "I don't know. A well-dressed man, not a drug addict, if a user could well afford to purchase his own, didn't want my money. I'd have sworn he was hell-bent on killing me, but he had ample opportunity. No, that wasn't his purpose either." Anderson eased his head back on the couch. "I don't know. I just don't know. I guess I'll call the police as I've always done in the past whenever my apartment was ransacked or my car was broken into. They never made any arrests then, and I have no confidence they'll be any more successful now, but I'd better call them anyway."

Anderson stared at Kate, a stirring in his loins. She was elegant in a Dior brown velvet skirt and a fragile cream silk blouse. In the delicate oval of her face, her eyes were midnight blue, wide-spaced, her mouth generous, with the faintest downward curve at the corners giving it a vulnerable look. Her ebony hair bronze and gold in the late sun was held in a loose knot at the back of her neck by a enamel comb. "Want to join me?" he asked.

"You're sure you're up to it?" Kate replied, half in jest, moving over to the sofa and kicking off her shoes.

Anderson lay face down and Kate started to work on his spine, pressing firmly with her thumbs, starting in the small of his back adroitly avoiding the discolored painful areas.

As she worked on his shoulder muscles, he could feel himself unwinding, breathing more deeply, less painfully.

Now her thumbs were on the back of his neck, near the area grazed by the bullet, pressing the tension out of it.

"Now turn around. Otherwise I can't get at your left side properly."

Anderson, feigning ignorance, complied.

Softly, he touched her and she arched toward him, helpless beneath his hands.

He clung to her, she to him. Each blissful within one another.

"We're good together." The words whispered.

Anderson's muscles tightened.

Kate kicked herself. She hoped she hadn't blown everything.

"He's tough," the Irishman barked into the receiver, "or he's crazy. Your way won't work."

"Did you get them?" the deep voice at the other end of the line asked anxiously.

"No."

"What happened?" His tone was two decibels higher.

"He doesn't scare easily, that's for sure. I fired several shots at him, even winged him once, but he kept on charging. He can certainly hold his own. There was no way to have gotten what you wanted without killing him. Since I was operating under strict orders—"

"That's enough. Does he know what you were after?"

"Not yet but I've been in this business a long time, have dealt with various types. He's smart. Sooner or later he's going to figure out what you're up to."

The older man breathed heavily into the phone. "Then do it your way. But, Steele—it must look like an accident."

Nine

Anderson gasped for air, helpless to push her away, unable to move.

Footsteps heard, muffled but there. Distant, deliberate, a set of shoes cautiously outside the door. In seconds, the figure of a man could be seen emerging out of the dim light. In his left hand, the stranger carried a small pencil light, in his right a long-barreled gun, swollen by a silencer.

Anderson tried to gain Kate's attention, to warn her, to give her time to escape, but she could not be distracted.

Anderson stared at this man now standing over them; there was something familiar about him, about the figure, the walk, the way he carried his head. What was it? What was it? He knew him.

But there was no time to think about it; there were two beats of silence, then an eruption of muffled gunfire, spits, and white flashes.

Blood splattering over the bed, a scream, then silence. All movement ceased. Anderson had to regain use of his muscles to free himself. He summoned his strength, still no movement. He glanced at her. What was happening? Two more shots came, Kate's head snapped back, her throat erupting in blood.

The man stood above Anderson, his eyes ablaze, his face contorted.

Then it registered. Anderson knew where he had seen the stranger. Two days ago. In his office. The realization came too late. Three shots exploded, ice like pain, streams of light. Then darkness.

"Stop it," Anderson roared. He tried moving his legs, his arms. They functioned. He could move. The pain was gone. Kate? Where was she? What was going on?

The doctor opened his eyes. He was lying on his back, staring at the dark wood that reflected the light of the night lamp by the bed. He slowly lifted his body, glanced bewilderedly around the room. Was it possible? Could it all have been a dream?

He raced to the bathroom, to the mirror. The left side of his neck covered by a bandage jarred his memory. An ironic grin crossed his face. It wasn't all a dream! He had been shot. Kate did come over. He remembered she'd driven him home, put him to bed, and left. That was two days ago.

Yesterday was spent recuperating from his injuries, listening to the news and waiting for McCormick's call, waiting to hear about Russell: anything, everything, instead nothing.

This evening he was to meet Kate for dinner. That gave him all day to wait and worry. The thought made him uncomfortable. He needed to know Russell's test results. He had waited long enough. He had to make the necessary calls and find out for himself.

He'd call Walter Reed, speak to Patient Information, and get Russell's number. No, that wouldn't work. They couldn't let anyone know the president was in the hospital.

Anderson reached for the note pad and pen he always placed on his night table and began listing people he knew that were on the hospital staff. A half hour later it was complete—as complete as his memory permitted.

He began the conversations quickly but casually and kept his ears primed to pick up any telltale sign in their responses. In each case his approach was the same; they knew he was a good friend of the president. He told them Russell was at Walter Reed, a routine checkup. That way no alarm would be inadvertently sounded. To a man, they were unaware Russell was in their hospital, but all volunteered they never were informed about the comings and goings of VIPs; that for reasons of national security the hospital's director, Dr. Aitkin, and the specific physician involved always maintained a strict code of silence.

The hospital director, Dr. William Aitkin. The name sounded familiar. Why? Then he remembered. Last spring, an unidentified middle-aged woman was admitted to the emergency room at New York Hospital, unconscious: drug overdose. At the time, Anderson was setting up a blood transfusion for a patient of his brought in with a bleeding ulcer. It was late. The staffing was inadequate.

Suddenly a whirlwind of activity. The woman sinking. Blood pressure inaudible. Anderson ran to help, began barking orders, directing the cardiac resuscitation. Twenty minutes later, the vital signs stable, he resumed working on his patient. The woman, Mrs. Adele Aitkin, had a long-standing history of alcohol and barbiturate abuse. Her husband, Dr. William Aitkin. At the time he was chief of medicine, Walter Reed. He persuaded Anderson to misplace her chart, that if it became known he had been prescribing for his wife's addiction, his career would be shattered.

It was time to call the favor in.

"It's Mike Anderson."

Dr. Aitkin's cheerful hello turned somber.

"I must know Russell's test results," Anderson said.

"Hold your horses. I don't know anything about the president being a patient here. Besides, even if he was, I'm not at liberty to discuss his condition with anybody."

"That's too bad. What about New York Hospital?" Anderson replied cynically.

Aitkin hesitated. "Let me double-check." He glanced at the list of doctors who currently had VIPs in the hospital. "As I said, McCormick hasn't admitted anyone this week."

"I'm aware of that. McCormick's out of town. He's using a neurologist."

"Oh, I see. Well, that would be Jason Bloom. Nope. He doesn't have anyone on the list either."

"Aitkin, check again. Go through your list from yesterday, from earlier in the week. It's doubtful, but maybe he was already discharged."

The silence on the line stretched for minutes. Mike felt his heart skip a beat.

"Anderson, I've checked everywhere. I don't know what you've been told, but according to our records, President Russell is not currently a patient at Walter Reed nor was he at any time this week."

Anderson placed the receiver in its cradle, conflicting emotions racing through his head. Russell not at Walter Reed, never admitted? How was that possible? Was Aitkin deceiving him? He quickly dismissed the thought as preposterous. Other explanations sought, all discarded.

He'd find out directly, call Russell, clear up the confusion. Further frustration. Anderson was informed the president was at an all-day meeting and had left word not to be disturbed. He'd call Peg. She'd know whether her husband had been hospitalized. Another hope dashed. Peg was out of town, not due back until late tomorrow.

One week ago, he had come so close to being free, his futilities in dealing with the normal world over. And now, seven days later, more involved than ever. But in what? That was the problem. He felt like an insect caught in an unknown spider's web. Russell, his best friend, demanding he drop everything, rush to the White House to find out what's destroying his ability to think. His fears understandable. But then roadblocks. Nobody cooperating. Russell wouldn't let Anderson hospitalize him, making the work-up exceedingly difficult. Peg either indifferent or too self-centered to realize how ill her husband was. McCormick, initially misdiagnosing the president, but after seeing the X-ray findings, willingly agreeing to hospitalize Russell. Yet now all indications pointed to Russell never having been hospitalized. Anderson himself a victim of an unidentified assailant. What the hell was going on?

McCormick, he'd have the answers. He had to get to McCormick. He glanced at his watch. Ten-thirteen, still early enough to catch Art in his room at the Plaza.

He'd call Art, inform him he'd be right over. No, on second thought, he'd forget about the call. If there was any chance McCormick was holding back, it would be far better not to warn him. But how would he get to McCormick's room? The switchboard operator wouldn't give out that information. Neither would the reception desk. Suddenly he remembered McCormick at the Oak Bar, playing with a key, a brass roomkey. He searched his memory. Eleven—eleven-something. He quickly pulled on a pair of blue slacks and a yellow sports shirt. Eleven-forty-three. No. Eleven-fifty-three. Yes. Eleven-fifty-three. That was it. He slammed the door behind him. McCormick was staying in Room 1153.

Saturday was reflected in the Plaza lobby, quiet and sparsely populated. There was one other couple in the elevator. Young, rich, pampered Manhattanites, fashionably dressed, lovers or newlyweds, aware only of themselves and their hungers.

The pair of hinged metal doors opened onto the eleventh floor corridor. Anderson passed tray tables of half-eaten food and the odor of coffee, the remnants of late breakfasts piling up outside the rooms. He tensed at the sight of a portly maid waddling by. She nodded, carrying towels over her arm. He gazed at the room number, 1153, and quickened his pace.

McCormick, dressed only in jockey shorts, watched her across the hotel room as she lifted the green skirt out of the box and folded it on her lap as though checking for imperfections. He understood that the pleasure he derived from buying her things was out of place. Clothes were a necessity, it was as simple as that, but he knew it did not erase the warmth that spread through him as he watched her. She never refused to let him buy clothes for her. McCormick had fine taste. Besides, she thought, her husband never bothered. Another example of why she loved McCormick. He pampered her. Nothing was too much for her. He used Judith, her middle name, never addressing her by her given name as if another name would erase the duplicity inherent in their relationship.

She kissed his cheek gently, feeling tender, close. The silence was interrupted by a loud knock on the door. "Honey, it's room service. I called up for your favorites, chocolate croissants. Please get the door."

The woman smiled lovingly and replied, "Hold your horses. I'm coming. I'm coming."

Anderson knocked again. That voice, he recognized that voice. For a moment he thought he should leave, turn and run before the door opened. Then he remembered his priorities, the reason he was there.

He heard the lock unfasten, saw the knob turn. He moved his gaze slowly upward and stopped speechless, staring in disbelief. Could he still be dreaming? Standing in front of him, wearing a fucshia-colored peignoir, was Peg Russell.

Anderson stopped, his breath suspended, a form of paralysis swept over him. His eyes didn't believe what he saw. He backed away, thoughts racing through his mind. Outrage paramount. How dare she? He stood motionless, words wouldn't come, wanting to scream, strike Peg, knock sense into her head. *Your husband may be dying while you're screwing your brains out!* He turned, dashed toward the nearby exit and headed down the staircase, his thoughts jumbled.

The whole episode had a déjà vu quality about it. The unexpected now commonplace. The Plaza steps, his mother; the loves of his youth. Now the cycle had come full circle. The Plaza, Peg Russell. He was a man running through an unfamiliar jungle inhabited by women playing games he didn't understand and couldn't win. The pain in his gut returned, knifelike, searing. What was it? Why did the pain come back?

Anderson momentarily lost his footing, fell three steps before righting himself, spun to the left to gain momentum and continued his descent, anger welling up within him. He wanted to lash out, blast Peg. How right he had been to seal himself off from women and their malignant lure. He never realized Peg was cut from the same fabric, not to be trusted. The image of her making love with McCormick sent ripples of nausea through his body, making him gag. He leaned against the banister, dizzy, his head throbbing. He had to force away these thoughts.

Russell was his top priority. Anderson had to find answers, the most crucial being to discover what was destroying the president's brain. What Peg wanted to do was her business. Who was he to moralize? McCormick was due to return to the nation's capital tomorrow. Anderson had to work through him, and to do that successfully he had to push aside today's shattering event.

One nagging question remained. Walter Reed had the most up-to-date medical diagnostic setup and one of the finest staffs in the country. What had caused McCormick to change his mind and not have Russell worked-up there?

She stood in front of him. He had not seen her come to him. Her whole body was trembling, she was gripped by fear. He couldn't erase her pain. "I'm scared to death he'll tell John."

McCormick held her firmly. "Believe me, he won't. Anderson's only concern is your husband's well-being. He won't jeopardize his health by upsetting him further."

Peg lit a cigarette, inhaled deeply, her hands still shaking. "I hope you're right. What kind of person am I to come here in the first place? John needs me now more than ever."

"Stop talking like a fool, Peg. We love one another. You and John haven't loved each other for years."

"I'm not talking about love. I don't know if I ever loved John, but I care deeply for him, I really do. I'd never want to hurt him. I should have listened to you and left him while he was still senator but that's out of the question as long as he's president."

She glanced forebodingly at her lover. "Why was Anderson here?"

McCormick saw in astonishment that her skin was chalk white. "I called him several days ago to help me with your husband. After all, no one has known Russell longer or for that matter better than Mike."

"But why did he come here without first calling?" Suddenly her eyes brightened. "Do you think it's possible he's come up with the reason John has gotten so clumsy and forgetful?"

"Let's hope so. I'll call him first thing Monday morning.

You've got to promise me one thing: that until I'm certain we know exactly what's what with John you'll emphasize to your father how critically important it is to maintain the news blackout. We can't afford to have a repeat of the paper's recent disclosure."

She nodded in agreement and reached up to him, her hands cupping his face, her lips inches from his. McCormick put his arms around her, pulling her to him, holding her.

"I tried to warn you, to warn us both," McCormick whispered as they moved onto the queen-sized bed.

They felt the fear and darkness sharply. But at that moment they chose to remain in the sunlight, if only for a while.

"What have I done wrong this time?" Kate asked, rubbing her ring finger around the edge of the wineglass.

"It's not you," Anderson replied tersely, his eyes suspiciously scanning those at Chelsea Place, studying the faces at the tables, looking for the inevitable: a pair of eyes, a glance behind a folded newspaper or above the rim of a coffee cup. There were several candidates; he couldn't be sure. A man at one table innocuously bringing a fork to his mouth. Would he be the one who would pull out a weapon powerful enough to blow him into the wall? What was coming over him? Why was he thinking this way? He couldn't live with this fear also. His inner fear was enough.

"Mike, you're running away. I can sense it. Please don't do this to me, to us."

Anderson's face turned expressionless, his voice flat. "Kate, I can't take these conversations. You've got to stop trying to change me. This is how I am. This is how I'll always be. When will you realize I like being this way?"

Kate promised herself she'd low-key it after upsetting him the other evening, but swelling frustration had diminished her resolve. Her father frequently criticized her for not rolling with the punches and changing tactics if need be. But that was her. Stubborn, pigheaded, rigid. Anderson was troubled. That much was obvious. But why and about what? She had to find out, even if the price proved considerable.

Kate bit into a piece of her steak au poivre with fierce determination. "Michael, you're hurting. I'm not going to shut up until you've told me why."

The pain in Anderson's eyes was made more acute by the flickering candlelight. "You don't know when you've pushed too far, do you? If I wanted to tell you, believe me, I would. Stop trying to be a mother."

"What kind of relationship is this? I can't watch the man I love flounder about. You're a doctor, you know talking helps."

"Now you're a psychiatrist?" Anderson replied sarcastically. "Cut it out."

Tears obscured Kate's vision. "If that's how you feel, maybe it's better if we don't see each other for a while."

Anderson answered abrasively. "You're right."

He waited for the pain to lessen and then disappear. Much to his surprise, it didn't. Instead, it increased.

Ten

It had become a daily ritual. Russell seated at his desk in the Oval Office, peering out the window at the line of citizens forming at the East Gate waiting for ten o'clock when the door would open for the guided tour of the White House. For two hours, the impressive state rooms would belong to the people. Russell received sustenance from watching them that helped him through these difficult days.

He turned to face the senior senator from Alabama seated on the leather-backed chair alongside his desk, looking like a blowfish, the ever-present cigar dangling from his overfed mouth.

"Thanks for coming, Cullie," Russell began. "I've been working on next year's budget. As you know, I campaigned on balancing the budget. To do that, I need your help."

"Mr. President, sir, we have known each other since you were a freshman senator. That's a mighty long time. We've been through rough periods and helped each other out many a time before. The two of us have gone a long way towards showin' those on the Hill how bipartisan support for the good of the country can and should take precedence over party loyalty."

"That's what I was hoping for. I can't balance the budget

unless you go along with my proposed cuts in defense spending and proposed increases for urban renewal."

"I'm listenin'," Cullie replied, a broad smile revealing two rows of sharklike teeth.

"In my inauguration address, I promised a new beginning, a fresh approach to problems, and offered the opportunity for some dramatic new steps. My speech apparently was perceived by the Soviet Union in the positive light I had hoped, for it led to the opening of channels between our two countries which I hope will culminate when Molonyn and I meet later this year." The president paused, poured a glass of ice water, took two sips, and continued. "To come to the point, Cullie, with this in mind, it becomes clear our budget is out of whack."

"What are you suggestin', Mr. President, sir?" asked Cullie, biting hard on the cigar butt.

"Cut defense spending. Cullie, we're overarmed. So are the Russians. There are no winners in a nuclear war. Everybody dies." The president glanced at Cullie's pear-shaped contour.

"What are your specifics?" Hamilton asked courteously.

"That's where you come in. I will recommend to Congress scrapping the proposed missile buildup program. That's a savings of twenty billion right there. But that's just the beginning."

"What do you mean, only the beginnin'?" Cullie frowned.

"For years we've given our military what amounts to a blank check. We've coughed up money for defense no matter what. No accounting, no checkups, no auditing. I'm going to put an end to that."

"What the hell are you talkin' about?"

"I'm recommending to the Congress we slash our defense spending by a third, thirty percent."

Cullie gasped, jowls flaring. "With all due respect, Mr.

President, sir, when you go, you certainly go all the way. This program can't pass. I can't possibly back you on it. The communists understand only one thing—naked force. All those on the Hill who stand for freedom and against tyranny will oppose you. That plan of yours is ill-conceived. You're right, balancing the budget is mighty fine. I'll back you on that one. But Congress will simply not tolerate such a capricious move as you're suggestin'. If I was you, John, and I mean this from the goodness of my heart, I'd rethink my position."

Hamilton's harangue caught Russell by surprise. He slumped down in his chair, drained, exhausted.

Cullie, noting the president's increased weariness, quickly seized the moment. "If I may be so bold, Mr. President, let me say your idea doesn't hold water. You've got to keep military spending in line with what we on the Hill, and I include myself in that group, demand. But, I'll tell you what I'll do for you. Have your meeting with the premier. If you come away from it with a document pledgin' nuclear disarmament, then I'll seriously consider presentin' your proposal to Congress. Till then, I think you're foolish to believe the Russians. I haven't trusted 'em for seventy years, and I haven't been proven wrong yet," Hamilton concluded, chomping his cigar in the corner of his thick lips.

Russell's eyes closed. With the strength ebbing from his voice he replied, "I would never contemplate such a move if I didn't fully believe we're at a point when the Russians feel as we do. It's time to plow money into our people and not into war machinery."

Cullie lit another cigar, the flame illuminating the bumps and ridges on his face. "Mr. President, my boy. I'll tell you what. I'm not goin' to argue with you. As I've said, I don't trust them Russians further than I can throw them, but if you'll get the damned premier to agree to disarm, I'll throw my weight around up there and do what you want done. I'll get them to balance the budget your way. Mr. President, I know I'm right in my thinkin'. You meetin' with them believin' Congress is ready to appropriate an increase in defense spendin' and you'll be in a better bargaining position than if you try it your way."

The president pulled himself straight up in his chair, turned, glanced out the window at branches from a nearby maple dancing in the breeze, and nodded. "Maybe you're right. I'll take you at your word. After the summit, I'll expect you to keep it. My budget must get through Congress."

"That, Mr. President, is a promise."

The Senate majority leader ambled out of the White House into a blast of hot humid air, his mind on how next to proceed, pleased with the manner in which he gently but firmly guided Russell away from his chosen path and down his own course. Hamilton had to continue steadily navigating, letting Russell believe he was steering the ship, playing on the president's unswerving loyalty and trust. *Cullie, you old devil you. Seventy and you still have the touch. Just a little more time, a few more twists and turns and come next summer you'll be a shoo-in for the presidential nomination.*

Russell felt only a sense of wariness, of futility. What had happened? When he called in Hamilton to enlist his support, he believed he had adequately prepared himself for the Southern senator's persuasive tactics. Why then had he buckled under Cullie's persistence?

If Cullie Hamilton was capable of wearing him down so easily, how could he proceed with the talks scheduled with the Russian premier? The thought of holding the summit in his present condition made him quiver. He'd be risking the future safety of the country. But it was too late to pull back now.

The president reached for the phone on his desk. Why

hadn't he heard from Anderson? Why hadn't the tests been done? Anderson was to have spoken with McCormick and arranged for the necessary work-up. It wasn't like Anderson to let things slide. What in God's name was going on?

Eleven

Soft melodious rhythms from the keyboard filtered through the various small private niches. Henry Jackson had purposefully chosen Dominique's for his important luncheon date, for he knew Kingsley preferred meeting inconspicuously and relished good food and wine.

Jackson believed himself to be a bright, clever creature cursed all his life by being six inches shorter than most of his fellow men. He compensated for this handicap by being overbearing and headstrong, at times to a fault. He was quite certain these qualities, coupled with petty jealousies of those far less talented, had prevented him from attaining the penultimate in journalism, the Pulitzer Prize. With these traits now harnessed, he felt confident the prize wouldn't elude his grasp this time around.

Jackson finished his martini on the rocks, crushed out his cigarette, and stared at his luncheon companion; the two of them were a study in contrasts. Jackson, the *Times* Washington Bureau chief, slight, forty-two yet looking fifty, florid, wispy, and lined, wearing a well-traveled gray suit. Bart Kingsley, the vice-president of the United States, appearing far younger than his fifty-five years would indicate, muscular, long-jawed with the crisp erect appearance of a career military officer. His brown three-piece herringbone suit a perfect fit. His shoes spit-polished, his personality matching: precise, methodical, demanding. Where Jackson tended to loquaciousness, Kingsley came directly to the point, never mincing words.

Jackson began. "I appreciate your taking the time from your busy schedule. I just wanted to say thanks for helping me out. My story about Russell's abrupt about-face on the abortion issue couldn't have come at a better time. I needed some kudos from the brass, and the piece did that."

Kingsley peered over his steel-rimmed glasses. "I know you better than that. If all you wanted was to thank me, you'd have called, not pressed for a meeting. What's on your mind?"

Jackson lit another cigarette. "For the past couple of months, the White House staff has been feeding the press corps quite well. That's not their style. Their pattern is to give a little: We push, they relent some, we question further. As far as I can tell it's always been that way, that is, until now. Suddenly the pattern changes. Feldman gives a thorough briefing on all matters we could possibly be interested in, fields our questions admirably, but then I notice something mighty interesting and start firing questions at him."

"Such as."

"Why has Russell, without warning, abruptly canceled our weekly press conferences and at the same time switched gears and stopped granting the press informal interviews? Feldman cleverly deflected these inquiries, so I got to thinking, and lo and behold, Kingsley, you'll never believe what I came up with."

"Get off it and come to the point," Kingsley said, unruffled.

"In due time." Jackson smiled. "You know exactly what's going on at the White House."

"I still don't know what you're driving at." Kingsley's reply had a soft-toned courtesy masking annoyance.

"There exists a wall between the president and the media. A barrier that hasn't existed before. I want to know why."

"That's preposterous. Nothing of the kind exists."

"Drop the upper-class routine, Kingsley. Your shit smells the same as mine. Something's brewing with Russell. What could be so important that all avenues to the president have been abruptly shut off?"

"I'm telling you you're off the wall. Eight years of being an investigative reporter have gotten to you. I'm Russell's right-hand man, his inner ear. That was our agreement before the election, and to this day he's kept his word, bouncing all his ideas off me." Kingsley fidgeted with his glasses. "You know damn well whenever anything newsworthy has happened I've immediately clued you in."

"I must say, you're right about that. But then why Russell's sudden reluctance to see the press?"

"It's unavoidable. He's been spending an incredible amount of time, much of it exasperating, in trying to fulfill his campaign promise to balance next year's budget."

"Do you think he'll be able to deliver?"

Kingsley leaned back in his chair. "I've never known Russell to fail in anything he's committed himself to, so I'm sure he'll iron out the details, and when he does I guarantee you'll be the first to know."

The significance of the vice-president's statement was obvious and required no comment.

Jackson ordered another round of martinis. "I've got some good news for you. Ginsberg's okayed the cover story on you for the Sunday magazine section. I thought it best if someone other than myself did the story. I don't want anybody to suspect you're my White House source. I believe you've met John Cohen. He's a good man and a top-notch reporter. He'll be calling in a few days. Ginsberg's set the story to run the first Sunday in October complete with a full cover photograph. The whole package should give you phenomenal publicity, so if you're right in your prediction that Russell won't run for a second term, you'll be starting the fall in view of the American public. A good place to be before the start of the winter primaries and next summer's nominating convention." Jackson paused. "As I said, one hand washes the other. You keep feeding me, and I'll do what I can for you."

Jackson waited for five minutes after the vice-president left the restaurant, then pushed aside the arrangement of orange marigolds and grabbed the phone line behind the floral display.
"Senator. I believe you'd like to meet. I have an interesting matter to discuss."
"Sounds mighty fine with me. If you're free I can make it for breakfast tomorrow. How's seven? At the Mayflower."
"See you then." Jackson quickly replaced the receiver in its cradle.
Too much was at stake to pin all his hopes on Kingsley winning the nomination and then the election. To ensure being the reporter who'd get first briefings on all fast-breaking news stories, he needed to gain favor with the man who most likely would oppose Kingsley in the November election. Now he had.
Jackson ordered a third martini. He knew he shouldn't but today was special and he wanted to celebrate. He lifted his glass to toast the two candidates: Bart Kingsley and Cullie Hamilton. May the better man win.

Anderson drove across the Chesapeake and Ohio Canal, the picturesque waterway separating the stridency of Washington from the tranquillity of the residential enclaves that made up

Georgetown, and entered the village whose quiet streets housed the wealthiest and most powerful men in the nation's capital. As he approached McCormick's residence, he heard a sudden swell of music bursting from the doctor's townhouse, filling the air and drowning out the sparrows. The soft, harmonious sounds of the Beatles' "Strawberry Fields Forever" were an ironic accompaniment to Anderson's dire mood. The ominous tones from Wagner's Ring would have been more fitting to the occasion, he mused as he parked his Avis rental and walked briskly up the brick steps that led to the porticoed entrance. He stopped at the white door, carriage lamps framing both sides, and knocked on the brass hardware, the noise momentarily overpowering the famed British voices.

McCormick swung the door open and stood motionless, his eyes boring into Anderson's. "You certainly have a knack for dropping in on me unexpectedly. Do you pull this on everyone or am I special?"

Anderson stormed by McCormick. "We both know why I'm here. If you're worried about my revealing your little secret—forget it. I've got more important matters on my mind. My big concern right now is my friend's conditon. I thought we had agreed you'd have Russell hospitalized at Walter Reed immediately after our talk. By the next day I began wondering what was happening. When you didn't phone, I became alarmed and called Dr. Aitkin, who stunned me by insisting the president was never admitted." Anderson paused and took a deep breath trying to contain his temper.

"Calm down. Relax, will you? Let's go into my study and talk."

McCormick led Anderson through the pristine white-walled foyer and into a small, richly furnished room of dark stained wood, brass, and expensive leather. Anderson glanced at the walls impressively covered with laminated diplomas and honorary degrees but he stopped scanning the imposing display after noting McCormick's current active duty status: major general in the U.S. Army. There was no need to add intimidation to his growing list of unresolved problems.

"You were right. He's tough. It was particularly hard from New York to persuade Russell he had to be hospitalized, that it just wasn't possible for the necessary tests to be done anywhere else. Just as I thought he was coming around, he threw up another roadblock. He agreed to be hospitalized, but not at Walter Reed. He said the place was too large, too many people, too great a chance for the media to find out he was there. If I could guarantee total secrecy, he'd go along. Otherwise, I could forget it. I pleaded with him. I told him how you and I were deeply troubled by his symptoms."

"What did he say to that?"

"He knew we cared, but it had to be his way. He said too much was at stake at this time to risk public exposure, and that we would have to accept his decision."

"What did he mean 'too much was at stake'?"

McCormick looked out of the large bay window, at the tree-lined street below. "You'll have to ask him."

"Do you know?"

"Yes, but not from Russell."

"From who then?" Anderson queried.

"I'm not at liberty to say. The whole matter is an extremely delicate one. Anyway, we've gotten off the track. I came up with a great solution, one that satisfies both our need to have the president hospitalized so we'd be able to run our tests and at the same time satisfies his demand that no one would find out about his hospitalization. I occasionally admit patients to a small private hospital in Virginia, not all that far from here. I don't have admitting privileges there, but a fellow I went to medical school with does. I presented my idea, and Russell accepted. He was in and out in three days. All tests done." McCormick smiled contentedly.

"What hospital?" Anderson asked curiously.

"Russell doesn't want anyone to know. I gave him my word. I know we're working on this together, but I can't betray his confidence. Besides, the evaluation is the important issue, and we'll share everything about that."

"We'd better," Anderson's business tone was firm. "What did the tests show?"

"They're not back yet."

"Not yet!" Anderson replied, waves of surprise spreading across his angular face.

"Listen, Anderson, I want to get to the bottom of this just as much as you do. Our timetable had to be pushed back because of Russell's demands. Leave me your phone number and where you'll be staying, and I'll call as soon as I know anything."

"No, I'll call you. The president is a walking time bomb. I can't simply sit around and wait."

McCormick walked quickly up the sloping lawn to the Capitol. The great dome towered above him against the deepening sky, shimmering, perfect, white, and pure over the city, over the nation. On the Senate side the flag waved lazily in the gentle breeze. If Cullie Hamilton hadn't summoned him with such urgency he would have felt utterly at peace, totally content on reaching the top of the hill for the day had gone beautifully, highlighted by regaining Anderson's trust.

He stepped energetically past the junior senator from Maine, nodding politely, and knocked on the Senate majority leader's door. A short, middle-aged receptionist with reading glasses waved the doctor in, Cullie by her side, cigar in hand.

"Thanks for coming. Miss Kelly, you see to it we're not disturbed. The doc here and I will be havin' a chat."

McCormick followed the pear-shaped figure into his spacious well-appointed office. "That there photograph you're lookin' at goes back a long time. That's me and President Ike Eisenhower handshakin' in Palm Springs after finishing a damn gruelin' eighteen holes." Cullie lit his cigar. "I sure looked dapper, trim and all, wouldn't you agree?" Cullie eyed McCormick. "Son, pull up a seat. I've got a mighty fine proposition for you."

The doctor eased into the soft upholstered chair, warily eyeing the senator, wondering what the cunning gentleman from the South wanted.

"You were mighty impressive at our little meeting the other day. You know I expect to be elected president of these United States next year and I could use a smart fella like yourself in my cabinet, say as Secretary of Health, or if you prefer an ambassador post, that'll be fine too."

"I've been in Washington for over two years, Senator. Why the sudden interest?" McCormick asked skeptically.

"It's really kinda simple. Till now I didn't need a favor."

McCormick was becoming increasingly uncomfortable at the direction the conversation was heading.

"You fill me in on the president's medical condition, maybe even treat his illness a wee bit more casually, mind you I'm not suggestin' managin' his case incorrectly, just perhaps with less dispatch. That's not askin' much in return fer what I'm prepared to offer now, is it?"

McCormick bolted from his seat, his face scarlet, veins pulsating. "Hamilton, with all due respect, you must be out of your mind. What kind of a person do you take me for? You can't seriously believe I'd betray Russell. I have a good mind to tell the president about your offer, but he's got enough to contend with as it is without burdening him further."

* * *

Seven minutes later behind the wheel of his green Audi McCormick smiled to himself. Yes, this had indeed been a most magnificent day.

Twelve

"A MAN FOR ALL SEASONS, ALL PEOPLES." THE PRESIdent turned toward Peg, his clear eyes shining as they always did, full of high intelligence, cold at first glance, yet somehow warmer the longer one looked at them, softened, perhaps by an understanding they shared. He continued reading the old edition of the news magazine he had found while rummaging through his bookcase. " 'This man, a man for all; transcending borders, languages, and national insanities. The world will either listen to John Russell's ideas or it will be blown to hell in a mushroom cloud.' " The president put the magazine aside, his eyes gloomy under a forehead drawn down. "Remember that article? Two years ago everything seemed possible, even probable."

Peg raised her eyes, alarmed. "John, don't talk like that. Nothing's changed."

"Stop kidding yourself. I'm not the same man I was when that story was written. My views haven't changed, but my endurance has. I don't have the strength to accomplish what I had hoped. It's that simple. My one regret is letting down those who counted on me, who believed in me."

"You're just tired. McCormick has been begging you to take time off, to rest."

"We've been through that. You know I can't."

"That's ridiculous, John. Two weeks away from the constant pressure, and you'll be as good as new, and have the energy you need for the summit meeting."

Russell tried unsuccessfully to muster a smile. "You don't want to face the truth. You were just like this when Dr. Curtin told you you'd never conceive, that we'd never be able to have children. You went from one world famous fertility specialist to another, not willing to accept their conclusions. Honey, wake up, will you? Look at me. I'm not run-down or tired. It's more serious than that."

Peg, noticing her husband's frustration, clasped her hand over his.

Russell looked up. "I've thought long and hard about what I'm about to say. It's the most difficult decision I've ever made, but I'm sure I'm right. Peg, after next year I'd like us to return to Virginia, back to Petersburg. These past years have been so busy, we've hardly had time for each other. I want to make that up to you. Our family house on the Appomatox River is waiting for us. We'd be able to live there, be together. What do you say?"

As the president spoke, anxiety crept into Peg's reddened face. Her eyes shifted their focus uneasily between the gray carpet and his pleading stare. "Politics has been your entire life. After a few months of fishing, you'd get restless. You wouldn't know what to do with yourself."

"Maybe you're right. But we both must face certain realities. It's best to say good-bye when you're still on top, and, Peg, I'm already falling."

"I know you believe that. I'm not going to try to convince you otherwise. I've watched you for the past several months, not pacing yourself, working eighteen-hour days in preparation for your summit meetings. I can't help but believe that the unrelenting pressure you've been putting yourself through has had more of an impact on you than you're aware."

"Exhaustion doesn't cause memory lapses and mental confusion. That's why I got in touch with Anderson." Russell glanced at his watch, and lifted himself from his chair. "I'm expecting Mike at ten. I hope he'll have some answers for me."

Peg, alarmed, drew her eyebrows together. Would Anderson dare tell Russell about her week in New York? She trembled at the thought. They walked in silence down the staircase and into the Oval Office, her body tense, her thoughts jumbled: a life in rural Virginia, a life without McCormick. She couldn't yield so easily. "You've always seriously considered my advice before making a decision. Now more than ever, wait on this one. After the summit, we'll get away for a few weeks. Just the two of us. We'll use Father's house in New Hampshire. You'll be able to ski to your heart's content. I promise if you still believe you're not up to running for a second term after that, I'll back you all the way. That will still give Kingsley enough time to gather the support he'll need before the convention."

Russell planted a buoyant kiss on Peg's lips. "That seems fair to me."

Her face brightened. She had bought herself more time. She wouldn't have to make up her mind, yet.

The sound of the buzzer caught them by surprise. "Mr. President, Dr. Anderson is here to see you," a high-pitched voice declared.

Russell smiled gently at his wife. "Don't worry. Either way, we'll be together."

Anderson entered the Oval Office. His eyes and Peg's made contact; it was brief and explosive. She steadied herself, staring at his face, his eyes, wondering what he was thinking, what he might say; then she furtively glanced at her husband. Did he sense the tension? If so, would he suspect its cause? The color ebbing from her face, she lowered her head and excused herself, lightly brushing against Anderson as she passed through the open door, realizing she had no control over what the two men would talk about. She'd have to rely on McCormick's assessment that Mike's friendship with John would override all else, at least for the time being.

Anderson stood arms akimbo, his breath escaping slowly; he was an uncertain man about to make up his mind. He knew he'd never tell Russell about Peg, but should he approach Peg in private and reassure her, tell her he'd never discuss her affair? As he reflected further, he decided against that option. He'd keep the matter to himself. Let Peg remain uncertain, let her agonize a while longer. Worry worked in strange ways. Some day the circumstance might arise where his secret would become a valuable weapon.

The president approached Anderson, his face flushed, the muscles of his jaw pulsing in anger. "It's about time you've come. Are you this nonchalant with your other patients, or, as a friend, do I rate special treatment?"

The doctor lowered himself into a nearby armchair. The president poured himself a drink and remained standing. "I didn't see any reason for us to meet until the test results were in." He looked at his friend. "How was your hospital stay?"

Russell rubbed his forehead, disbelief in his eyes. "What stay?"

Anderson gulped hard. Was it possible for Russell's condition to be deteriorating so quickly that his memory was fading this rapidly? "I just left McCormick. He told me you were in a private hospital for a few days and had the necessary tests run."

The president studied Anderson with perplexed eyes. "Where was this hospital?"

"Some place in Virginia. McCormick told me you asked him not to reveal any specifics."

"What hospital? What tests? Are you serious! I've been in this office all week working on that damn budget."

Anderson's stomach dropped. "You mean you haven't been hospitalized and haven't had the tests done?"

"I don't know what McCormick's told you, but I haven't left the White House."

Anderson climbed to his feet and walked slowly towards the drawn curtains, parting them, looking absently outside. "You're leveling with me. I believe that."

Russell spun Anderson around, fear gripping his body. "Could I have been in a hospital, actually had those tests taken and totally forgotten all about it? My God, I am losing my mind."

Anderson stared at the president, speechless, unable to reassure his friend.

Outside the Oval Office, Anderson leaned against the wall, bewilderment and concern in his look, further questions on his mind.

Peg stood in the passageway. "Can I speak to you for a moment?" The words clogged in her throat.

An icy stillness descended over Anderson's manner, disguising the confusion within.

She stared at him, her hands trembling, her body shaking. A physical reaction like this had happened to her once before, while at school. Five hundred girls lining the gymnasium wall. The headmistress in the middle, everybody waiting for the culprit to confess. Her knees gave way, and she sank to the floor. The doctors called it hysterical paralysis. A week later after it was positively proved she hadn't been the guilty one, her symptoms lifted. This time it was different. Standing in front of Anderson, legs like putty, she knew she was at fault, deserved to feel ashamed.

"I know what you must think, but please believe me, Mike, I've never done this before. It's not as if Art and I are having an affair, we've been together for years."

Anderson bore in on her. "Well, what are you going to do about it?"

"What do you want me to say? I don't know what to do. I don't want to hurt John, especially with the way he's been feeling. I care very deeply for him, we've shared so much together. But I love Art."

He gazed at her moist eyes. "I never liked McCormick. Now I can't look at him without wanting to puke."

"It's not his fault. I could have resisted, said no. I didn't."

Anderson, resignation in his eyes, replied, "Look, Peg, somehow I've got to shut this out of my mind, otherwise I won't be able to work with Art, and if I'm to help your husband, I must do that." Michael paused for a moment. "At times I believe McCormick is deeply concerned about Russell's welfare, that he's a conscientious and devoted physician. Yet at other times, I sense he's indifferent and not involved. It's confusing as hell. I may need your help."

"What you're saying about Art is absurd. He's been very concerned about John from the beginning."

Michael's impatience rose. "Fine! Just remember I may call on you for a favor."

"Would that be in return for your continued silence?"

"Yes."

"What kind of favor?"

"If I begin to suspect McCormick is undermining my attempts to properly diagnose and treat John—"

Peg interrupted, "I can't believe you're serious. You're sounding like a detective."

"I didn't say McCormick is doing anything wrong. But if I become suspicious, I want to know I can count on you."

"Do I have a choice? You tell me what to do, what to find out, and I'll do it."

The president was plowing through a stack of files on his desk when Kingsley arrived. They moved to one of the couches near the fireplace and Russell ordered drinks. Their conversation remained casual until the butler brought the tray.

"That fellow who just left. He looked familiar. Who was he?"

"Mike Anderson, an old friend."

"Ah, yes. If I remember correctly, he's a doctor, isn't he? Was it a social call?"

"Not exactly. I've asked him to help McCormick."

The vice-president shook his head. "I don't think that's a wise move, John. We've done a pretty good job of concealing your, uh, your situation. McCormick knows the political arena, he's adept at dodging potentially damaging questions. But with Anderson involved, an innocent statement eagerly grabbed up by an ambitious reporter or a power-hungry politician, an accidental leak, and you're ruined. All your efforts over the years for nothing. I've told you about Hamilton's secret committee. Fortunately, I chair it, but my control goes only so far. Its purpose is to discredit you, to prevent your summit meeting."

"Bart, you know I wouldn't jeopardize our country. That's why I called in Anderson. I trust him. If he determines I shouldn't meet with the premier, I won't. I'll call it off."

"I believe you. But as I said, I have limited control over the committee. So far so good, thanks in large part to McCormick.

I've never given you bad advice. John, leave Anderson out of it."

"Let's drop it," Russell said sharply. "What else is happening on the Hill? Are the boys in line?"

"Everything's fine on that score. Just keep staying away."

"Bart, I appreciate what you're doing. I'm sorry I lost my temper." The president rubbed the tension from his neck. "As we agreed, you get me to the summit, and two weeks later, regardless of how I feel, I'll announce my decision not to run again. I'll get those in my camp to support you. The presidency will be yours."

"Thank you, Mr. President."

The rain had cooled the air, the night sky an impenetrable blanket, dense clouds obscuring the moon.

Georgetown, usually bustling with evening strollers, was empty, the eerie quiet interrupted only by the rain pounding on the cobblestones.

Ragland cursed himself for agreeing to have drinks with Jack Keyser at Martin's Tavern this evening. He was busy enough without agreeing to help Keyser raise funds for Yale University's capital campaign drive. He glanced at the dashboard clock, eight-forty-three, climbed out of his car and into the deluge. He was running behind schedule. He'd have to hurry Keyser along and then race to La Niçoise for his nine-thirty dinner with McCormick. Ragland was eagerly awaiting the opportunity to have it out with the doctor. After the scene in front of the Capitol, he was certain McCormick would move quickly, but he had been mistaken. Unanswered telephone calls, further delays, additional rationalizations. Ragland had had it. Nothing was being done to find out why Russell was behaving erratically. He'd give McCormick an ultimatum: One week, or he'd make certain Russell replaced him.

Suddenly a powerful light came from his left, burning his

eyes, blinding him, followed by a heavy flashlight smashing down on his hands. A strong arm shot over Ragland's shoulder, vising his throat in a hammerlock. Pain spread over his crushed hands as he was dragged into the deserted alley. The hammerlock briefly choked off Brent's air as the heavy metal crashed down repeatedly on his hands. As the blood burst from the back of his left hand, he twisted his fingers, letting it flow between them until both hands were covered. He fought back the urge to scream, the grip lessened; he shouted, "My hands. They're broken." The left was damaged to the point where it was useless, but not the right. He moved the fingers, wincing in pain. "Who are you? What do you want?"

The barrel-chested attacker kicked Ragland in the groin, then tore at his clothes, ripping his shirt. Then, as unexpectedly as the beating started, it stopped.

Ragland gasped for air, frightened, his body quivering. He stepped forward. The stranger threw the flashlight down and reached into his pocket. "Toss your wallet to the ground," he said, jamming the barrel of a gun into Ragland's chest.

Brent slowly raised his bloody right hand, grabbed his wallet, and flinching with pain thrust his wallet onto the pavement.

The stocky man holding a modified Smith & Wesson M-39 bent down to retrieve the object, then stood up.

Relief swept over Ragland. A robbery, that's all it was. Neither man moved. Three minutes passed.

"You're free to go," the thief barked.

Ragland spun around and began running.

Slowly, the muscular man raised his automatic and fired, the bullet exploding inside Ragland's skull.

The realization he had been fatally shot came with his last wheezing breath.

Thirteen

RAILINGS OF GOLDEN OAK, MARBLE FIREPLACE WITH ornate wooden mantles, fancy embossed ceilings and shimmering stained glass windows. The Fourways Restaurant, near DuPont Circle, was a facsimile of Sagamore Hill, Theodore Roosevelt's mansion in New York's Oyster Bay. Large tables, adorned by Villeroy and Boch china, were filled this noon with many of the city's powerful.

Henry Jackson in his rumpled gray suit rose to greet his competitor. "Ah, Dawson, good to see you. I took the liberty of ordering your favorite, mousseline of bass, and a carafe of white wine."

Eric Dawson nodded and sat down. The investigative reporter tugged at his starched white collar, noticeably tighter around the neck from frequent banquet excesses. "It's a shame about Ragland. Found beaten and shot to death like that, and in Georgetown no less. Nothing's sacred any longer."

"Any thoughts?" asked Jackson, his condescension obvious.

"Just idle speculation. And you?"

"Very confused. Too messy for a professional job. According to the medical examiner, he was savagely attacked and then killed. Wallet was missing, so I'd bet on robbery."

Dawson sipped the wine. "Good Chablis. I don't know if I

go along with that." He turned to his pale colleague. "We both know Ragland's been going out of his way to shield the president from us. It will be interesting to see how the White House will handle this one. Do you think Russell will dare continue his low profile? I tend to doubt it. Everyone knows they were buddies. If Russell stays out of the limelight, then there'll be no denying something screwy is going on there."

Jackson picked up his fork and speared a piece of bass, letting it drip sauce onto his plate before he leaned forward and took it into his mouth. "We chose a mighty peculiar way to earn a living. We're rewarded by others' misfortunes. The greater their calamity, the better our dessert."

"Wouldn't it be great if something big came out of Ragland's murder? It wouldn't be the first time an obvious tragedy had far-reaching implications," Dawson replied hopefully.

"I counted on your saying that. I know you've condemned my methods, but this administration keeps such a tight lid on what it disseminates that unless we work together, share information, and pool sources, neither of us will get anywhere."

"Our bosses would never agree."

Jackson interrupted, wiping a piece of fish from the corner of his mouth, "Where is it written we have to tell our publishers?"

"I never thought of that." Dawson hesitated, took another sip of wine, "It's just—"

Jackson cut in again, "That's why the top stories pass you by. Ethics and reporting don't always go hand in hand."

Dawson eyed Jackson dubiously. "You're a piranha. You've never cooperated with anyone before, why now?"

"I've never had to. I'm not suggesting we collaborate fully. We're not allies. I'll feed you whatever I uncover, and I expect the same from you. Other than that, I'll do everything possible to nail down the story first."

They shook hands, a verbal agreement, and rose to leave. Dawson glanced casually around the restaurant; recognizing four senators, three congressmen, and a Supreme Court judge scattered throughout the room. He wondered what other clandestine deals were being consummated.

Dawson crossed Twentieth Street NW, searching for a taxi, his subconscious mind at work. If he waited trustingly and patiently, it invariably came up with answers. At least one that might work. Certainly, the surest and quickest way to get facts would be to contact Ragland's secretary. They had met at Senator Clark's farewell reception last spring. He'd taken her number, implied he'd call.

Suddenly a different thought began germinating, slowly growing, pushing aside his first plan. He remembered seeing a photograph of three men holding up a large fish. One was Ragland, the second Russell, but the third. Who was he? Whoever it was would be the logical one to question, a friend of both men. With a carefully planned interview he might be able to find out not only crucial facts about Ragland, but more importantly, information related to the president and why he had dropped from public view.

Where had he seen that photograph? A taxi came to an abrupt halt, the driver blasting his horn, startling Dawson. The reporter quickly opened the rear door and slid inside.

It was during an interview. A two-hour question-and-answer marathon with a doctor in Manhattan, part of his critically acclaimed series last year on insurance fraud in the medical community. A four-part series dealing with doctors, their fees, and hospitals, their costs.

His conclusion, in large part based on the doctor's answers, was revealing: Patients' bills were frequently tied to their insurance coverage and were not an accurate reflection of the costs involved.

Who was the doctor? Dawson had interviewed only five for the series. He could see him clearly. He tried placing a name with the face. Then finally, the perfect fit. Anderson. That was the doctor's name. Dr. Michael Anderson.

Ecstatic, he jumped from the cab. A once-in-a-lifetime story. Jackson was right. Dr. Anderson had better be prepared. Scruples be damned.

Russell, facing Peg and Michael, sat on one of the Bellangé chairs in the Oval Blue Room. The formality of the French Empire style in the drawing room served to hold their emotions in check.

The president was pale, his voice hoarse and somber. "Just like that, thirty years rubbed out. A meaningless act of violence. I don't know what I'll do without him. From the start he's been like my right hand, sacrificing all. Never married, totally devoted to me, and my career." Russell turned towards Peg, seated alongside Anderson in one of the other gilded beechwood chairs. "We shared everything. I don't recall any decision without him present. He even helped me select our wedding rings."

Peg, at a loss for words, glanced at Anderson, hoping he'd be a comfort. The doctor, staring straight ahead, lost in thought, remained quiet.

The president stood. He seemed suddenly to have shaken off the shock that had subdued him. "Did you see the editorial in this morning's paper?" The president, not waiting for a reply bent down and lifted the paper from a table and began reading.

> Brent Ragland will be remembered as one of the best press secretaries in any recent administration. His warmth, sincerity, and easy availability will be greatly missed. The role he filled was made more critical by the president's reluctance to engage the media. His successor, not to be envied, has quite a pair of shoes to fill.

The manner of his death will require the publication of certain facts about his life that might otherwise have been known only to a few Washington insiders. The fact was, Press Secretary Ragland was frequently seen with young women. The motive for his murder may be found in his private life. Superficially, robbery seems a sufficient cause. However, the possibility exists he was killed by a jealous lover. The brutality of the slaying makes it less likely the crime was perpetrated by a woman scorned. The police will have to look into this aspect of the story unless they come up with the killer very soon.

Anderson slowly rose. "What ridiculous innuendos. Journalistic muck, that's all it is."

Russell joined Anderson near the fireplace. "That's not the point. This administration, any administration, rests on trust. Destroy credibility, and you're left with nothing. Ragland's life is now an open book. Unless we meet the issue head-on and find out some answers, we're asking for trouble."

"What do you suggest?"

"I've already met with Harrison from the FBI. I've given him Ragland's telephone log, his desk calendar, his appointment book, his secretary's telephone log and calendar. He'll be working together with the Metropolitan Police Department," Russell paused, "Mike, I want you to be my liaison with Harrison, meet with him and report back. Putting politics aside, as friends we owe it to Ragland both to find his killer and clear his name."

Anderson nodded acceptance.

Russell walked towards the mantel, glanced at the Pearsall and Embree bracket clock. Eleven-fifty-three. Then seeing his reflection in the gilded looking glass above the mantel, he straightened his tie. "We've got to get a move on. We've only seven minutes until the press conference."

A worried expression crept over Peg's face. "Are you sure

you're up to it? You haven't faced them for over two months. It'll be grueling."

"I don't believe I have a choice. Not showing my face is tantamount to admitting something's wrong. This way the entire country will see I'm in control. Any rumors to the contrary that have been circulating will be squashed."

Anderson voiced his concern. "What about your memory lapses?"

"Hold on, both of you. Neither of you give me any credit." The president reached into his pocket and pulled out a sheet of paper. "I dictated the message I'm going to deliver. All I'm going to do is read what's typed here, then excuse myself and turn the session over to Kingsley. Everyone will understand my grief over Ragland's death and will think nothing of it. Bart will field all questions." The president, clasping his hands over his head, smiled, "I think you'll agree I've covered all contingencies."

The president had selected the East Room for the news conference because he needed all the dignity his office and the mansion could provide, and the Cabinet's chamber fit the bill perfectly. The portraits of John Quincy Adams and George Washington looked down on the television cameras, radio microphones, and excited reporters.

It was an expectant crowd assembled on the chairs, brought into the East Room when the decision was made to hold the conference. With few exceptions, nobody present had seen the president for the past few months.

Ladies and Gentlemen, the President of the United States.

Kingsley followed Russell into the East Room and took a chair at the table where the president stood and faced the microphones. He was the only other person at the table.

"As all of you know," Russell said, speaking softly and slowly from his notes, "Press Secretary Brent Ragland was found dead late last night in Georgetown, apparently beaten and murdered. A very thorough investigation is presently under way. The Secret Service, the FBI, and the Metropolitan Police have worked all night. As of now, they haven't any suspects."

Russell's face glistened with sweat, his voice strained. "Before continuing, I want to say that Brent Ragland was a very close friend. He was a man of outstanding ability, energy, and loyalty. Both as president and as friend, I am determined to find out who killed Ragland and why. With the coordinated efforts of all our investigative agencies, I'm confident the murderer will be brought to justice."

The president paused, glancing at Kingsley. "At this time, the vice-president will answer your questions."

Before Russell had a chance to leave the podium, a loud, deep voice bellowed. "Mr. President, please. One minute of your time."

All eyes turned towards the large figure standing in the center of the crowd. The president was caught off guard. If he turned the meeting over to Kingsley, needless suspicion would be aroused. He had no choice but to respond.

"Mr. Coleman."

"I'm saddened, as I'm sure all of us are, by this senseless killing. Ragland was a remarkable press secretary and a wonderful person. We'll all miss him. But, Mr. President, if I may, I have a question. It's been rumored through the grapevine that your budget proposals for the next fiscal year are in place and we're in for some surprises. I'd like you to comment on whether you have indeed gone against your campaign pledge and slashed the programs to revitalize the cities and to educate the poor. And if so, how, Mr. President, can you justify such a drastic turnabout in policy?"

The president's body stiffened like a rigid marionette uncertain of its strings. He leaned heavily against the podium, wrestling with the question, attempting to organize a response. His right arm began shaking, his hand felt numb. He slowly opened his mouth to answer. Nothing. Silence. Words wouldn't come.

McCormick, quickly summoned, had reassured the journalists. Russell had become emotionally distraught, a common occurrence given the circumstances, and would be fine within the hour.

Exactly sixty minutes later, the president briefly appeared to appease the lingering skeptics. Satisfied, they disbanded.

Anderson, sprawled out on the queen-sized bed in his hotel room at the Lee House, a small homey spot conveniently located four short blocks from the White House, wasn't so easily comforted. He knew today's symptoms didn't augur well for Russell's future.

The jangling from the antiquated phone box on the night table continued for several rings. Finally Anderson lifted the receiver. "Yes, this is Dr. Anderson. Who is this?"

"Eric Dawson. I interviewed you last year."

"Oh, yes. I thought your series was quite good."

"Thanks. I heard about Ragland's death and wanted to pay my respects. I remembered you were old friends."

Anderson, startled, replied, "How'd you know that?"

Dawson chuckled. "You had a photograph on your desk. I saw it during our interview. There you were, alongside Ragland and President Russell. The three of you holding up quite a hunk of fish."

"Why the call?" Anderson inquired guardedly.

"No sense beating around the bush. Ragland's death is an incredible story. I though you'd be able to shed some light on his murder."

"Sorry, but I can't help you on that score. I only know what I've read in the paper."

"Is that so," Dawson said sarcastically. "You were involved

in a messy altercation yourself rather recently, weren't you? Attacked and beaten in your office, I believe."

Anderson registered surprise. "How'd you know about that? It was kept out of the newspapers."

"You reported the incident to the police, I have my connections at headquarters. It's really very simple."

"What made you call them?"

"That photograph on your desk. It made quite an impression on me. Three friends: one behaving for the past few months like a recluse; another just murdered. I began to wonder if anything unusual had recently happened to the third. So first thing this morning, I flew to New York and spoke to my contact at the Nineteenth Precinct, your precinct. I asked him to run a check to see if he had a file on a Dr. Michael Anderson, and lo and behold, bingo. There it is, clear as daylight: three good friends, one killed, one attacked, and the other in hiding."

"I still don't follow."

"That's why you're a doctor and I'm an investigative reporter. Coincidences don't sit well with me. I believe a connection exists that'll explain what's happened to the three of you, and I plan on finding out what that link is before—"

Anderson interrupted. "You have an incredible imagination."

"Think whatever you wish, but I've been at this business a long time and I trust my hunches. Something is going on with Russell. For your sake and for Russell's I hope you'll let me in on what it is, before it's too late. I'd hate to pick up the morning paper and read that your body was splattered over a city street or that it was found floating in some polluted river.

"Think it over. I can be reached at the paper day or night."

Part Two

Fourteen

UNDERSTANDING AND PATIENCE, NOT TALENT OR IN-genuity, Kate Robins realized, were at the heart of her success as she pushed herself between the two talented craftsmen. The brief flare-up of tempers subsided. The tall slender man stood momentarily erect and let forth a scream of invectives in French. His much younger, stockier adversary made a sullen comment about the other's ancestry. Kate, gentle and firm, gradually led them back to work. These winning qualities, shown in her career, were curiously missing in her personal life.

Her studio, a third-floor loft overlooking Horatio Street in Greenwich Village, light-years removed from the chic sophistication of her showroom located in the glass-and-steel D&D monolith uptown, was a hornets' nest of activity. She had promised to have her new design based on the curves of the eighteenth-century French rococo style ready for next month's international furniture show in Brussels. But three weeks of frenetic eighteen-hour days had not brought her innovative concept to fruition. It was now August 18. She was rapidly running out of time. Thoughts about Anderson kept intruding and distracting her. It had been several days since they'd seen one another. Why hadn't he called?

Kate bent down, carefully eyeing her creation, satisfied with its stylized appearance. The back, arms, and frame of the chair formed a continuous whole, the difference between the supporting and nonsupporting parts concealed.

Her last task, upholstering the chair with a French country print, remained to be done. Stepping over wood shavings, she strolled through the wide room, the light sluicing down from spotlights overhead. Frustration and apprehension arose within her as she reached her desk and glanced at her phone. She had to fight back the impulse to dial Michael, to reassure herself he hadn't forgotten her.

She wanted to settle down, she thought to herself, and not with a chair, regardless of the security and comfort it provided. How easy it would be to call Michael, his need for space be damned. What about her needs, didn't they count? She clutched the phone, thought better of it, and reached into the top drawer of her desk, pulling out a brownie and devouring it. Her glance shifted from the telephone to the drawer with the brownies and back again. She grabbed the receiver. Damn. She'd only be replaying the same pattern. She gobbled down a second brownie, tapped her manicured nails on the receiver, and began dialing.

The phone rang. In the middle of the second ring she abruptly slammed the receiver down. No, she wouldn't go through with it. He'd have to make the next move. She shoved a third brownie into her mouth. Kate could only hope he'd call before her skirt split.

"Russell swears he never was hospitalized; you insist he was. I don't know what to think," Anderson said bewilderedly.

McCormick leaned back in his chair before speaking. "I can understand your confusion, but bear with me. Everything will become clear. Unfortunately Russell's comments are consistent with our findings. I'm sorry for the delay in getting the results done and the frustration it's caused, but he set the ground rules. I didn't see where I had a choice. I had his records photocopied today. Take a look."

McCormick handed Anderson the president's folder. "Better prepare yourself, it's not good."

Anderson stared at the manila folder. He had pushed McCormick into action. Now he had to confront the truth. His eyes wandered from the files across McCormick's Georgetown office: a cluster of three small rooms that, unlike his impressive quarters at Walter Reed, he used when privacy was paramount.

He couldn't bring himself to open the chart. "It's a brain tumor, isn't it?"

McCormick sensed Anderson's reluctance. "I wish it were. A brain tumor lends itself to hope. Surgery, followed by a course of radiotherapy and chemotherapy. Many are cured, others go into remission. No, it's far worse. It's what Russell's always dreaded."

Anderson adjusted his body into the corner of the chair, fixing his eyes on the chart, trying his hardest to subdue his emotions. Russell's nightmare had become reality. He had Alzheimer's disease, a progressive illness that would leave him a vegetable. Those sleepless times in college, his morbid fixation through the years, his feeling doomed. Russell had been right all along. How could it be? His best friend wasting away, Anderson helpless to reverse the inevitable process.

He took a deep breath, attempting to regain his composure. "Let's see the X-rays."

McCormick snapped the pneumoencephalogram into place. "As you can see, the ventricles are significantly larger than normal, indicating a sizable decrease in brain tissue." McCormick then pointed to a faint circular shadow that covered the brain surface. "While these X-rays are always difficult to read there's the definite sense that air has infiltrated and begun to replace the normal tissue."

Anderson picked up the folder, and began flipping through the pages, periodically stopping to absorb its contents. Ten minutes passed, his dismay growing. Finally in disgust, he flung the chart, the papers scattering, onto the rosewood desk. "I was hoping the blood tests might point to one of the reversible forms of dementia but"—he paused—"there's no question about it. It's Alzheimer's."

McCormick replied, "Of course, to be a hundred percent positive, we'd have to perform a biopsy, remove brain tissue and microscopically locate neurofibrillar degeneration and senile plaques, the two features pathognomonic to this particular dementia."

"Let's not, these tests are conclusive enough. Whatever we'd accomplish putting Russell through that torture would be strictly academic, it wouldn't alter his future one iota," Anderson replied.

"I'm totally in agreement. I think you can now understand Russell's response to your question. He's already forgotten he was hospitalized. These memory lapses, as we both know, are only going to get progressively worse with each passing week."

"What do you plan on doing?"

"I'm going to talk to Russell. He's got to know the score and what to expect. He's got many important decisions to make, and he must make them while he's still able."

"How far along is he?"

"I spoke to Dr. Parks, at Mass. General. He's the country's leading authority on dementias. He believes these tests show Russell is still in the earliest stage of the illness, and that while the end result is inevitable, proper rest, good nutrition, and eliminating stressful situations wherever possible should allow him to continue functioning, at least for a while. More than that, he couldn't say."

"Will he be able to complete his term?"

"I doubt it. He'll likely get through this year. Next winter as well. After that it's probable he'll have to turn the presidency over to Kingsley. But as Dr. Parks emphasized, there are so many unknown factors in Alzheimer's. The rate of deterioration varies considerably from patient to patient, so maybe Russell will be one of the more fortunate and go downhill very slowly. If that's the case, he'll be able to complete his term. I just don't know, nobody does."

"I take it that regardless of its progression a second term is out of the question."

"Absolutely," McCormick stated emphatically.

Anderson walked toward the viewboxes and stared at the pneumoencephalogram. The loss of brain tissue was undeniable. His eyes remained riveted to the screen while his mind wandered. Suddenly his memory was jolted. What about the results of the skull X-rays? His portable series had shown a shift in the pineal gland, a finding inconsistent with Alzheimer's.

A modicum of hope stirred, he turned to McCormick. "I'd like to see the skull films."

"Be my guest." McCormick shrugged his shoulders. "I know what you're thinking. Forget it. There was no shift in the pineal gland."

Anderson studied the X-rays. "I don't understand. In the skull X-rays I took, there was a definite shift in the pineal."

"Dr. Zaslow, who took these during Russell's hospitalization, said portable X-rays, especially of the skull, are frequently inaccurate, often quite fallible, and can lead to misdiagnosis. He repeated the series four times; the results were identical. Regardless of the angle, the pineal remained dead center, directly midline, without a trace of a shift."

Anderson's fleeting optimism vanished. "Russell asked me to find out what was wrong. Now that we know, I'd like to break the news to him; I owe him that."

"By all means. He's going to need all the support you can give him. I don't envy your position. I'm sorry, very sorry for both of you."

Anderson, stunned, stood in the street directly below McCormick's window, breathing heavily. His best friend in the ultimate labyrinth, soon to know he was racing blindly, that there was no escape. The diagnosis had been made, was irrevocable. There could be no bargaining, for its certainty was established.

The light changed. Anderson broke into a run. He had no time to lose. He had to make sure he spoke to Russell before his courage ran out.

McCormick looked out the window at the shadows rushing past, watched Anderson as he slid into his car and disappeared in the distance, heading directly into the heart of the nation's capital.

He moved away from the window, gathered the X-rays, flicked off the viewbox, picked up the papers strewn across the desk, organized Russell's file properly, and then carefully placed the chart in his lower desk drawer, tucked away under numerous medical articles, hidden from any unexpected view.

He lit a cigarette, drew in deeply. He was satisfied with the way the meeting had unfolded. Everything conceivable had been taken care of. The diagnosis had been made, the treatment plan established, the prognosis was dismal. He believed that Anderson, now distraught, with the passage of time would eventually accept the findings. Then the two doctors working together would help Russell salvage whatever time remained.

Anderson believed that they were allies engaged in a common battle against the same deadly enemy. That had been McCormick's goal. He had pulled it off successfully. The recent worrisome days could at last be pushed aside. He broke out laughing until tears of relief and tiredness ran down his cheeks.

All was back under control.

Fifteen

Streams of sunlight danced blithely through the room, the buoyant rays in marked contrast to the gloom that enveloped both men. The three-minute walk down the drive, into the West Wing, and along the chaotic, humming corridors to the Oval Office hadn't been sufficient to prepare Anderson for the flood of emotions that threatened to overwhelm him. He had planned on unfolding the findings gradually, softening the eventual blow. Cushioning painful medical facts this way made eventual acceptance easier. He'd always been able to handle this delicate matter successfully with other patients, but the closeness of his relationship with the president wouldn't allow it.

Russell perceived the agony in his friend's face. "It's about Ragland's death, isn't it? I still can't believe he's gone. My staff's pushing me to appoint the new press secretary. They're right, of course, but I can't bring myself to do it. Tell me, what has the FBI come up with?"

"That's not it," Anderson replied, looking away.

"Then come out with it. Something's eating you."

"I was with McCormick. He showed me a copy of your hospital transcript."

"Then you weren't joking the other day."

"No. There's no doubt you were hospitalized. . . ."

Russell interrupted. "And I've no recollection of it. None whatsoever. My memory is really going, isn't it?"

"I'm afraid so."

"Then I have to know everything. All the details. Whatever came out of my hospital stay. Don't leave anything out."

"I don't have to. You already know it all," Anderson muttered, slumping down on the nearby couch. "You've been there before."

Russell sat alongside Anderson. "My father?"

Anderson nodded.

"But that's impossible. He couldn't do anything. I can function. Sure, I've become forgetful, but I'm getting older. Maybe McCormick was right. A few weeks rest, and I'll be as good as new."

"You've never conned yourself before. Don't start now. You told me to find out what was wrong. I have."

"I spent all these years worrying about getting Alzheimer's. You know what, deep down I never believed myself, I never thought I would." Russell sighed. "Go ahead. I won't interrupt."

Anderson carefully revealed the findings, elaborating where necessary, omitting nothing. He ended by repeating verbatim his conversation with McCormick.

"So there's a good chance I'll be able to finish out my term."

"That's not what I said. Count on six months, no more. And that's if you take it easy. After that, the everyday stresses of the presidency will be too much to handle."

Russell glared at Anderson. "And if during these six months a crisis should develop?"

"I'm not an expert on Alzheimer's but . . ." Anderson stopped in midsentence.

"You were going to say something. Go on, spit it out."

Anderson continued hesitantly, "I don't think even now you're up to dealing with a critical situation."

The president sprang from his chair and began pacing. "Mike, you don't understand."

"Understand what?" Anderson had no idea how long he sat there, in silence, his eyes glued to his friend. Finally Russell threw his arms into the air, clenched his fists and in a rage born out of helplessness smashed his knuckles against the desk. "Damn it! Why now? The timing couldn't be worse."

"What are you talking about?"

The president sat down next to Anderson, tapping the rug nervously with his right foot. He began speaking quietly. "I'm in a difficult position."

Anderson's voice rose. "I'd say you are. I've just presented you with a death sentence."

"No, it's more than that."

"John, I don't understand you. What's more important than your life?"

"My word."

"You trusted me enough to involve me to this point but—" Anderson got up to leave. "If that's the way it is, I'm afraid I can't do anything more. I can't help with one hand tied behind my back."

"Hold on, Mike. This has nothing to do with friendship. I'd like nothing better than to tell you. You'd be able to answer some very important questions."

"Then tell it to me as your doctor, not as your friend. That should relieve your conscience."

Russell leaned back on the couch, took a deep breath and replied. "Premier Molonyn and I have agreed to hold a secret summit conference on disarmament before the end of the year. If the reason for it should be disclosed, any possibility for reaching accord between our nations might be lost." Russell stared at his friend. "Now, you see my predicament?"

"Very clearly."

"I have to be able to function effectively during my meeting with Molonyn. If I can do that, I'm confident we'll be able to hammer out an agreement that will lead to bilateral nuclear disarmament. It's what I've been striving for. After we sign the treaty, I'll resign from the presidency, content with my accomplishments."

"That's quite a goal you've set for yourself."

"If only I didn't have this illness, I'm sure I could achieve my goal. What are the chances my mental state will deteriorate too much before then?"

"I don't know. But the sooner you hold your meeting, the greater the chance you'll be in a position to pull it off successfully."

Russell leaned over and embraced his friend. "Thank you. Thank you very much. I'll meet with my aides. We must come up with a way to convince Molonyn that the sooner the summit is held, the better for all concerned."

After the events of the past several days, Anderson wanted a stiff drink and left word at the reception desk that he could be reached at Durdy Annie's, the hotel's popular turn-of-the-century pub.

Now, seated on a leather bar stool, downing a double martini, he was deep in thought; the crowd of attractive women and handsome men with their polite laughter went unnoticed. His nerve endings were raw. Ragland dead, Russell dying, and that gnawing ache in his gut intensified by Kate's explosion. He ordered another double martini, gulped it as quickly as he had the first and had started to request a third when the piercing ring of a nearby telephone interrupted him. The bartender nodded into the receiver and dragged the phone line towards him. "It's for you."

What now? Anderson thought. "Yes?" he said into the receiver.

"It's Fred Harrison. I've got news about Ragland. I'll be at the FBI building until five. Can you get here by then?"

"I'll be right over," Anderson replied, the feeling of helplessness returning.

At the far corner of the long bar, a stocky, middle-aged man sipped a cold Coors beer and continued an animated conversation with his blond, well-endowed companion while out of the corner of his eye he watched the doctor leave the pub. He stood up, excused himself and gently brushed against his friend's overflowing breasts. She had turned him on, but he'd finally been given the go-ahead to proceed. He had to squash the impulse to make it with her, at least for the time being. Later, who knew? But, for now, business had to take precedence over pleasure.

Harrison's office served him well. His six-foot-four presence complimented the huge brass-studded desk that had dwarfed his predecessor. The walls of the vast room were brought closer by the bookcases that rose from floor to ceiling. On a shelf beside Harrison were two photographs in heavy gilt frames. One was instantly familiar to Anderson: J. Edgar Hoover, the first chief of the FBI. He peered discreetly towards the other.

"That's me, a bit younger and shall we say less filled out," Harrison explained, approving of the doctor's curiosity. "Take a seat, Dr. Anderson. We've turned up something interesting. Ragland has a kid. He's eleven and lives in Bakersfield, California."

Anderson was stunned.

Harrison leaned back in his large, upholstered chair and smiled. It was apparent he relished digging up potentially embarrassing information. "Needless to say, the kid's a bastard."

"So, the newspapers were right. Ragland was killed because of his love life."

"No, we don't think so. Oh, he had many affairs, some quite intriguing, but we're pretty sure he wasn't killed because of any lady friend."

Mike looked surprised. "Then why was he murdered?"

"We went over his log on the day he was killed. Did you know he was on his way to meet Dr. McCormick when he was murdered?"

"No."

"Were they close friends?"

"I don't know, but I wouldn't have thought so."

"Why do you say that?"

"They're different types. Ragland is—was—outgoing, warm, very friendly. McCormick is aloof, hard to reach, really quite standoffish."

"According to the phone company, Ragland called McCormick's office three times that day."

"Brent told me he didn't like McCormick's nonchalant attitude. That if he was to be the president's physician he'd have to jump when ordered."

Harrison looked up from his papers. "Three calls that day to arrange a dinner meeting in order to discuss an attitude problem. Doesn't that strike you as odd?"

Anderson didn't know if Harrison knew about Russell's condition. He decided to play it safe. "No, that was Ragland's style. He'd invite you for dinner and after a few drinks launch into an attack. You'd be amazed at how effective his approach was. Any further mistakes and you were out, no explanations accepted. You'd had your chance to atone and had blown it.

Russell loved it. He left these matters to Ragland, confident they'd be handled well."

Harrison shook his head, admiration in his eyes. "You're very convincing. You must have one hell of a bedside manner." He reached into his vest pocket, pulled out a pair of bifocals, fitted them over his hawklike nose, and looked down at Ragland's log. "We think we're on to something. Ragland received four calls the day he was murdered from a man who, according to his secretary, had a thick Irish accent, called himself Jack Keyser and needed to see the press secretary to discuss some kind of capital campaign fund for Yale University. She thinks they were to be cochairmen of the drive. Anyway, I called New Haven, got Keyser's phone number, and called him. Get this, he hasn't seen or spoken to Ragland for over ten years and has never gotten involved with any type of fund raising. To top it all off, Keyser is from the Midwest and doesn't have a trace of an Irish accent."

Anderson leaned forward in his chair, not knowing what next to expect.

The bulky head of the FBI continued, "One of my agents stopped by Keyser's Chicago office yesterday and had a long talk with his secretary. It seems our friend with the accent called Keyser's office the day before Ragland was killed, requesting to speak to Mr. Keyser about an important matter. He told the secretary that several years ago Keyser helped a friend, Dave Paley, out of a really bad situation. Our caller must have only wanted to make sure Keyser was still working in Chicago, since he said he'd call back rather than be kept on hold. Needless to say, he never did."

"I don't follow."

"Dave Paley has been implicated in many big-time schemes. We have a two-inch dossier on him. Once we almost had him, but Paley pulled a real coup. He retained Jack Keyser as his attorney and Keyser convinced the grand jury to dismiss the case on the grounds of insufficient evidence. Our files show Paley has frequently enlisted the skills of a top professional to do his dirty work. His name's Steele, Brian Steele. Mr. Steele is the proud owner of a pronounced Irish brogue."

"You're linking this fellow Steele to Ragland's death!"

"Yes," Harrison replied, eyes brightening. "We succeeded in tracking him down. He was in the Washington area the night Ragland was killed."

Anderson's respect for Harrison suddenly grew. "A news reporter I spoke to doesn't believe in coincidences."

"He's a smart fellow," Harrison said, pressing down forcibly on his palms and lifting himself from the chair. "Brian Steele, one of the country's most notorious hit men, was hired to kill Brent Ragland. We've got to find out who hired Steele and why!"

Sixteen

RAGLAND MURDERED BY A PRO, ANDERSON THOUGHT as he passed the deep green maple tree across from the FBI building. The jolt cut through the numbing effect of the afternoon's alcohol. Anderson climbed into the dusty rental and turned on the ignition. He had to get away, to escape from the growing chaos that was encircling him. Maybe he'd return to Durdy Annie's and lose himself once again in booze. He continued along Pennsylvania Avenue, narrowly missing a pedestrian wandering too far from the curb. The attractive woman triggered thoughts of Kate Robins. Her soft, comforting voice, somebody who cared, who he could open up to. No! He couldn't give into the temptation. He had to fight the urge. She was part of the agony. He'd drive to Virginia, explore the countryside, unwind, and think. With speed and luck he could get to a motel along the Shenandoah Mountain Range before dark.

Anderson felt the knot behind his neck loosen. He began to focus on the recent chain of events, on his two friends.

Ragland had died as he had lived, dramatically and unexpectedly. Russell, fighting for survival, was struggling against the severe blow fate had dealt him, driven to get the most from each remaining day. How, Anderson wondered, could he have allowed himself to become so self-indulgent, so self-centered, so filled with remorse and self-pity that he wasted days contemplating suicide? Maybe he had more than his share of blows, but where was it written life was meant to be fair? He had given up to avoid hurt. Could he have been wrong? After this nightmare was over, should he consider the possibility of risking again and perhaps, through risking, feeling alive? He didn't know. He'd have to wait and see.

Anderson drove the Citation to Route 33 at Hinton and thirteen minutes later was traveling on Route 629 through the Washington National Forest, part of the Shenandoah chain. He relished the serenity of the back country road with its rounded curves and sparsely populated valleys. A few hay and milk trucks came cautiously out of dirt roads, speedy cars overtook him intermittently, salesmen who had covered the day's territory, racing to the next motel. In his six-cylinder Chevrolet, he knew he couldn't outrun those slick streamlined imports.

A bright beam of light shot out from the encroaching darkness. He could see the outline of a car behind him in the wide convex mirror outside the window, the image magnified by the curvature, its shiny grille immense. The vehicle was coming closer. He recognized the familiar emblem on the hood, heard the roar of the engine; it was a turbo-charged Mercedes. Anderson released his foot from the accelerator, his car slowing. He waved the Mercedes on. The image grew larger, then steadied, the German vehicle keeping four feet behind, not passing. Must be a crazy teenager out for some thrills, Anderson thought, jamming his foot on the accelerator. The Chevrolet lunged forward.

The Mercedes kept pace effortlessly. Michael glanced at the speedometer. The needle wavered at 70, the car shaking. The cars on the other side of the road were a blur. There were two trucks up ahead. They followed one another around a long curve in the road. He passed them and tried to get away from the lunatic following him. He stabbed the accelerator, turning the wheel counterclockwise, swinging to the left side of the road, the engine thundering as he sped past the two trucks, stunning the drivers, the Citation wheels half off the pavement, the tires screaming. Quickly he spun the wheel clockwise, swinging back to his lane.

He looked out the rear-view mirror. His plan hadn't worked. The Mercedes was approaching rapidly, its grille growing larger. He braked, the car slowing to a crawl. He pulled off to the side of the road and waited to see what the Mercedes would do. It came to a halt directly behind the Citation.

Now what? Anderson thought, his breathing fast and erratic as if he couldn't get sufficient air into his lungs. He snapped up the handle and leaped out. He raced over to the Mercedes and grabbed the door handle, pulling with all his strength. The door was locked. He pounded on the window.

"Who are you? What are you doing?"

The impassive face stared straight ahead behind the glass. There was no acknowledgment whatsoever.

Anderson shook the handle and smashed his hand against the window. "You crazy bastard! Who are you? What do you want?"

The face, that terrible pale face, turned and stared at him. Instant recognition. It was the man who attacked him in his office.

I don't believe in coincidences, Dawson's words reverberating in his head, their impact frightening. Dawson's instincts had been right. Anderson, always the hunter, was now being hunted. He'd obviously been followed, his every action monitored. But why?

His eyes darted in both directions. No cars approaching, no way to flag for help. Somehow he had to get to the next town.

He had passed a sign: DEERFIELD 5 MILES. That was about a mile back. That left four miles before he'd be able to lose himself in a crowd, four miles to safety.

Anderson ran back to the Chevrolet. He threw himself into the seat and slammed the door, his fingers slapping the lock. The motor was still running. He reached for the gearshift and pulled it into drive, his foot hard on the accelerator, his hand on the wheel. The Citation exploded in a burst of power, Mike gripped and swung the wheel to prevent the car from jumping the curb. He straightened it out and sped up the road.

It was a nightmare. Why hadn't he rented a faster car? His Citation was no match for the power of the enemy. The car climbed the steep hillside. Behind him, he saw the yellow glare of headlights probing into the darkness.

Anderson continued gripping the steering wheel, the muscles in his arms tense. The Mercedes maintaining a steady pace, never more than ten feet away, the headlights blinding in the rearview mirror.

His pursuer was not going to close the gap between them. Not then. Not at that moment. He was waiting, waiting for something. But what?

Then he knew. A sign up ahead: ELEVATION 3,760 FEET. He heard the roar of the engine behind him and felt the sharp pain increase in his stomach, followed by the jarring of contact, metal against metal as the car behind hammered into the Citation's left rear chassis. Anderson lost control, the wheel spun, tearing his arm. His attacker struck again, crashing into the left rear fender, breaking the fender and jamming it through the left rear tire, all air escaping. The car reeled off the pavement, then off the road, and suddenly it was lurching and skidding down the rocky mountainside. It continued its rapid descent, a large tree directly in its path. Anderson, frantic, spun the steering wheel to the right, avoiding a head-on collision, the tree ripping the left front of the car. The radiator burst. Steam roared loose under the hood. A headlight broke and went out. The windshield shattered. The left front fender broke loose and rose up like a specter of torn metal. He had to stop the car before it rolled over. He forced his foot down on the brakes. The car continued sliding. The brakes wouldn't hold. The Citation was tipping over.

Anderson smelled something. It was gasoline. The gas tank had been damaged. Gas was leaking. He had to get out before the car became a blazing inferno. In desperation, he reached for the door handle, trying with his other hand to steady the car, prepared to jump if need be. The lock jammed. He couldn't get out.

Time froze. The Citation began tumbling faster down the mountain. Then an explosion filled the air, the blinding light bathing the darkness of the woods, echoing throughout the countryside.

From above, the stocky man pulled alongside the edge of the road and stared downward at the mushroom cloud of reds and oranges. He wanted to stay, wait for the fire to die out, inspect the wreckage, and see Anderson's charred remains. But it was safer to leave, curiosity unsatisfied. Oncoming cars, neighbors in the area might have heard the noise. Their lights would pick out the skid marks on the road for the surface had been badly torn. But even if they guessed that some accident had happened, a tire suddenly blown out or a turn too sharp and too quick, they could see little over the precipitous edge. It was too steep, too deep, and the night was too dark. There could be no salvage party until daylight.

Brian Steele got back into his car, took off his jacket, opened his shirt collar, and reached for the telephone under the dashboard. "The job's done. He's dead."

Seventeen

"I CAME AS SOON AS I GOT YOUR MESSAGE, MR. PRESIdent," McCormick said, shaking Russell's outstretched hand.

Russell poured them both a drink and handed McCormick his glass with a faint half smile. His bushy eyebrows stood out starkly over hollow eyes; the deep furrows and bags under his eyes were obviously due to lack of sleep.

"Anderson and I met yesterday. He hit me with everything. What do you think?"

"That it's a damned good thing you called him in when you did. At first I resented his intrusion, but of late I've gotten to respect both his ability and his thoroughness. I can't believe how off the mark I was. Seeing you as often as I did caused me to overlook the subtle changes that to Anderson were so glaring. His prodding finally paid off. Fortunately, as I'm sure he told you, you're still in the earliest stages of the illness, so that if you pace yourself properly, you'll be able to keep the signs dormant. Only a trained eye will be able to spot anything unusual in your behavior."

"And the summit?"

"Ah," McCormick paused, surprised at the question. "I

didn't realize Anderson was aware of your intentions. What was his opinion?"

"The sooner I hold the meeting, the better off I'll be."

"I agree. Mr. President, I don't mean to be presumptuous. As I said, I admire Anderson greatly, but I believe he's frightening you unnecessarily. You'll be able to handle yourself quite competently at the summit."

Russell eyed McCormick skeptically. "The medical profession has always confused me. Presents one problem, winds up with two different approaches. The difference in your attitudes is very troublesome. It makes it difficult to decide on the wisest course to follow."

McCormick finished his drink, sloshed the ice cubes against the sides of the glass and replied, "You know what they say about the doctor who treats a member of his family: that he has a fool for a patient. Well, with all due respect, Mr. President, you and Anderson border on that boundary. He cares so deeply for your welfare, he's overly involved emotionally, not able to maintain the necessary distance to allow his scientific objectivity to hold sway. Hence we both see the same picture, but I'm able to put forth a more rational approach. Believe me, you have more time, a great deal more time to work with than Anderson conveyed."

Russell's eyes brightened. "I know you're right. I see the pained look on his face and hold back on telling him about certain symptoms. I find myself protecting his feelings much as I do Peg's. Doing all I can to minimize their worry."

"This causes you to become far more apprehensive than is indicated. Mr. President, let me guide you over the next several months. Confide in me. Let me worry. You have enough to do. I'll make it a point to drop in every morning before you are to start your day, we'll talk, I'll go over you thoroughly. This way we won't miss a thing. Let me in on everything and I promise the summit will be a success."

* * *

"Peg!" McCormick called, recognizing the figure at the far end of the West Wing. He quickened his pace. The figure stopped and turned, her middle finger in her mouth. "Not so loud," she whispered.

"Can we go to your study and talk?"

"No, that'll only arouse suspicion. I'll walk you to your car. We can talk on the way." She turned to face McCormick. "Art, John has decided not to run for a second term."

A Cheshire grin spread across the doctor's face. "Peg, that's great. You'll be a free woman. It's almost too good to be true. We'll finally be able to be together." He gazed down into her lovely taut face. "Why do you look so glum?"

"I was happy for a while, but then I began thinking. The way John has been feeling lately I couldn't leave him even if he wasn't president. I'd feel too guilty. He needs me now more than ever. I couldn't abandon him unless he was well. I'd never be able to live with myself."

"Do you know what you're saying?"

Tears welled up in her eyes. "Yes, unfortunately I do. I'm married to a man who, although he denies it, is very sick. Each day he seems to be getting worse. At times, it's as if he's becoming senile. Am I right? I want to know the truth."

McCormick regained his composure. "Please don't worry. He should be fine, especially if you'll help me."

"How?"

"Convince your husband to listen to my advice. I need to monitor his condition very closely. If he lets me do that, I can steer him through his crucial talks with the Russian premier."

"And after that?"

"With that burden lifted, I should be able to determine his condition quite accurately. I'm confident he'll pull through just fine."

"I'll make sure he cooperates with you. I hope to God you're right and he will regain his health. Only then could I leave him."

McCormick looked into Peg's tear-filled eyes. "Just get him to follow my orders and everything will work out."

"I will," Peg said, wanting desperately to throw her arms around him. "Art, I love you so."

McCormick smiled warmly. "Then trust me."

Kate collapsed wearily in the armchair behind the desk, looking through the half-glassed wall of her office. Her showroom, less than an hour ago overflowing with the hum of the media, was empty now except for caterers gathering their wares and a porter tidying up the premises.

After today's extravagant media event, orchestrated by Kate's public relations firm, vast numbers of magazine and newspaper readers as well as television viewers would now recognize Kate Robins as one of the top furniture designers of the late twentieth century. She had always valued anonymity, but with her talent receiving critical acclaim her name would shortly be a household word. There was no turning back. The years of painstaking frustration were behind her. She could sit back and bask in the glory, perhaps even enjoy her fame. That was the American way, wasn't it? But she couldn't. She needed somebody to share her success with, otherwise she felt her accomplishments were meaningless.

Why could she grab the reins in her career yet not in her personal life? Whenever she had tried being passive, she lost out. Why then had she taken that path with Anderson? To hell with waiting for his call. She had waited long enough. She might lose him this way but that was the chance she was going to take.

She lit a cigarette and dialed Anderson's home. No answer. She quickly rang his office.

"Dr. Anderson's office," a perky voice answered after the fourth ring.

"I'd like to speak to the doctor."

"He's not in right now. Give me your name and number, and he'll get back to you."

"Tell him Kate Robins called. He knows the number."

"Oh, Miss Robins, I didn't recognize your voice. I saw you on the five o'clock news. I never realized Dr. Anderson was seeing someone so famous."

Kate, momentarily taken aback, paused for a moment. "It's important that I get in touch with him. Is there a number where he can be reached?"

"I'm afraid not. Dr. Anderson has been away for the past several days. He was due back this morning but so far he hasn't called in. I don't know where he is."

Kate gulped hard. "Has the doctor ever done this before?"

"Not in the eleven years that I've been taking his calls. He's usually most conscientious about these matters. He's the doctor I'd go to see if, God forbid, I ever took sick."

"It's strange he didn't leave a number where he could be reached," Kate replied.

"I'll tell him you called, and Miss Robins, good luck with your career."

Irritation and annoyance vanished, replaced by alarm. Her mind racing, facts analyzed, absorbed and discarded as rapidly as they came to her. She lit another cigarette, her hands trembling. One incident remained vivid. Anderson being attacked and beaten. The more Kate thought about the episode, the more convinced she was that something had happened to him.

She had to find out, but how? She racked her brain, searching for a solution. She didn't know any of his friends or colleagues. It had always been just the two of them. A sinking feeling gripped her as she realized she was all alone, with no one to turn to.

Eighteen

A PINPRICK AROUSED HIM.
"He's coming to. Dr. Anderson, can you hear me?"
The voice sounded faint and unclear as it echoed above his head.
"Dr. Anderson, move your right arm."
The command clearer. The tone firm and direct.
"Dr. Anderson, open your eyes."
A different pitch, softer with a gentle resonance, a woman's voice. This order understood. Why these commands? Where was he?
He struggled to open his lids, white blurs beside him slowly coming into focus.
Anderson felt pain. It seemed to be all through his right side. He rolled his head, feeling the pillow beneath him. A tall elderly man in a long white coat stood beside him, the veins in his slender hands pronounced. At the foot of the bed, two women, both young, also in white, one tall and dark, the other short and fair, stared at the wrinkled man, as if they were robots awaiting direction.
"Ms. James, I want you to stay and take a detailed history. Ms. Murphy, come with me."
Anderson watched as the two mysterious figures left the

brightly lit room. He shifted his head and tried to raise himself on his left shoulder, pushing his elbow into the mattress, his right side painfully following the turn of his body like a dead weight.

"Be careful," Ms. James cautioned gently, her long black hair pulled back, revealing small delicate features.

Anderson reached over and tugged at the band of adhesive tape that held the intravenous line in place on his right forearm. "Where am I? What am I doing here?"

"Please, calm down. One question at a time. You're at Clarkson Hospital, in Deerfield. You've had a nasty accident. For a while it was touch and go, we thought we were going to lose you, but your body wouldn't give up. Dr. Wheeler just gave his nod. He's the best, and when he gives a patient that signal, it means the danger point has passed."

Deerfield. The name hurled him back in time. He remembered a sign, then darkness filled with violent noise, crashing metal and his body twisting, spiraling into the black void. Oh, God. How long ago was it?

"How'd I get here?"

"Warren Simmons, a state trooper, was passing by on his way home and noticed flames coming from down the mountain. Lucky for you he stopped, saw a car on fire, and you lying unconscious twenty feet from the burning wreckage. He had you here within twenty minutes." Ms. James pointed to Anderson's bandaged right fist. "You had some nasty gash on your hand. Mr. Simmons believes you smashed your way through the front window, managed to pull yourself to safety and then passed out. There's a sharp curve right where your car went off the road and you did have some alcohol in your blood. So Simmons figures you overshot the angle and headed down the mountain. As I said, you're damn lucky. The fire was spreading through the woods. Another five minutes, and you'd have had it."

"How badly hurt am I?"

"Nothing's broken if that's what you mean, but you've been unconscious for four days. Now that you're awake Dr. Wheeler will be able to evaluate your head injury. But he doesn't think you've done any permanent damage."

A half week gone from his life, irretrievable, lost forever as if those days never existed. If he needed further proof it wasn't time to pass over to the other side, he now had it. He shuddered at his abortive suicide attempt. It wasn't time to die, rather to live, to regain control over his life. He only hoped his assailant agreed.

Anderson glanced at Ms. James as she recorded his vital signs. "Let me read my chart, please."

The nurse reacted with a mixture of surprise and scorn. "You're a doctor, you know that's out of the question."

Anderson backed off. "I'm sorry, just thought as a doctor I'd be allowed to see my own records."

Ms. James shook her head. "No. It's hospital policy. We don't allow patients including doctors or nurses to read their charts. We respect your privacy, never look at anything you write, and we in turn demand the same."

"That's absurd! I only wanted to find out what went on during the four days I was out of it. Can't you make an exception? It's very important."

Ms. James replied, a hint of irritation in her words. "The answer remains no. You're a physician, you know darn well many things said to us never would be if confidentiality wasn't guaranteed. Here at Clarkson, we go so far as not to give out information about our patients, even to concerned relatives, unless the patient has signed a written authorization allowing us to do so. I know we look like a small, nothing hospital to a city man, but we get our share of famous people who come here for, shall we say, a rest. They don't want to be disturbed and we do our best to grant their request. No, Dr. Anderson, as long as you're the patient, you'll have to live like the other half do, listening to orders rather than giving them."

A gurney passed through the hall, carrying an emaciated man, the ashen pallor of encroaching death surrounded him. "Look, I've got to get back to work. Get some rest and I'll be back in the morning to get a thorough history." She forced a smile. "Otherwise, Dr. Wheeler will have my neck."

Michael propped himself up in bed, wincing at the pain in his right leg. They wanted to know his history. To hell with them. He knew it only too well. What he didn't know was the extent of his injuries, the X-ray report, the results of the lab tests. These he needed to see in order to assess his physical condition, to determine how long he needed to be hospitalized, how long he'd have to wait before it would be safe to sign out against medical advice. To wait to be discharged was a luxury Anderson couldn't afford. There were too many questions that couldn't be answered as long as he remained in the hospital.

Fifty minutes passed. Timing was of the essence. The nurses were in the midst of their eleven o'clock personnel change. They'd be in their lounge, not in the nurses' station. If he wanted to grab his chart, this was the perfect opportunity.

Anderson struggled to get up, finally managing to perch on the edge of the bed, his feet touching the floor. A wave of lightheadedness came and quickly passed. He ripped off the adhesive tape, pulled out the I.V. line on his right forearm and squeezed his arm with a bedsheet until the bleeding stopped. Slowly he lifted himself from the bed, pain shooting through his right temple, spreading downward, curving in his neck and throbbing at the base of his skull; sharp but bearable. His gate unsteady, he positioned his left arm against the wall to maintain balance as he inched toward the open door, peered out into the corridor and with halting steps edged forward. He listened to the clamorous silence of night in the hospital.

The sighs and coughs. The moans and labored sonorous respirations. He passed darkened rooms, the patients locked in their own struggles, a fight not for wealth or happiness but merely to survive and return to their lives. A searing pain shot through Anderson's right leg. He looked down. It was swollen. The sutures, hidden by bandages, began pulsating. He had to take the weight off the leg. He increased his pace. The nurses' lounge was buzzing with activity. He had guessed correctly. It was the change in shift. Eight nurses, six from the outgoing group and two from the new shift, seated around a table covered with papers, coffee cups, and ashtrays were giving their evening report and wouldn't notice him walk by.

The nurses' station loomed straight ahead, brightly lit, empty. Anderson supported himself on the wall and favoring the stronger leg, hobbled to the station's large central desk. The charts were kept in a circular stainless steel file built into the countertop. With his left hand, he began to turn the chart rack slowly until he came up with the chart that had his name taped across the front.

Anderson braced himself against the cabinet and began reading, quickly flipping through the nurse's notes, studying the admission entry and physical and then racing through the lab results looking for the skull X-ray report. He found it and methodically deciphered each word. "No body abnormalities present, no evidence of subdural hematoma or skull fractures. Diagnosis: Concussion." Satisfied with the report, he was returning the chart to its lodgings when his right leg gave way. Fighting to regain his balance, he lost the grip on the chart, the metal record holder smashing against the desk and falling to the floor.

Maxine Boyars, the night charge nurse, had left the nurse's meeting early and was pouring out medication in a treatment room when she heard the noise, hesitated for a moment, then stuck her head into the chart area. "What are you doing here?" she said, her eyes bulging. "This area is off limits to patients."

Anderson stared back at the matronly shape. There was nothing to say. He had found what he was after and was relieved that he'd be wheeled back to his room. The pain in his right leg was becoming unbearable.

Eight minutes later, back in bed, side rail snapped in place, I.V. running, the nurse scowled at Anderson. "You'd think a doctor would have more brains than that. You're on strict bed rest. That means no toilet privileges, let alone wandering the hall in the middle of the night, snooping through your chart. You should be ashamed of yourself. Dr. Wheeler gave us orders to sedate you. Take this."

She handed Anderson a fast-acting sleeping pill, Tuinal, and a glass of water.

Reluctantly, he swallowed the pill. At least he'd sleep peacefully knowing there was nothing seriously the matter with him and that he'd be able to leave the hospital in a few days.

Anderson's eyelids were getting heavy, starting to close, the TV on the wall was becoming hazy. Lying on his back waiting for the barbiturate to lull him to sleep, he began thinking: not about Russell, Ragland, or even the attempt on his life. Rather, his mind focused on his chart. There was something disturbing, something he had seen in his record. He tried forcing himself to concentrate, to think. What had it been? His head fell back into the pillow. It was no use. His thoughts dulled, the Tuinal was overpowering. He submitted to the pill's sedative effects.

Anderson awoke with a start, fully alert. The spill from the sodium lamps outside the window separated him from total darkness. He reached for his digital watch lying on the nightstand, 4:12 A.M. Thank God Wheeler had ordered a fast-acting barbiturate. He was only out for four hours. With one of the longer acting preparations it would have been late morning before he'd come to and an additional two hours before he'd be able to throw off the drug-induced hangover.

His mind flashed back to his chart. Something puzzled him, something about the X-ray report. What was it?

Suddenly the realization. Dr. Zaslow. The name of the doctor who read his X-ray and the radiologist who read Russell's were one and the same. He visualized Russell's hospital chart and his own, all lab reports and other tests. They were typed with the same typewriter and on identical paper. He sat up in bed, his heart pounding in his chest. There was no doubt about it, Clarkson was the hospital McCormick had admitted Russell to.

Anderson wondered if there was anything in Russell's hospital chart that McCormick hadn't shown him. Was there any chance the doctors were in error in their diagnosis, and that his best friend was suffering from a curable ailment rather than Alzheimer's? There was only one way for Anderson to find out. He had to get his hands on Russell's chart. He knew Russell had probably been admitted under a false name. That meant he had to remember the unit number. He recalled seeing the number when McCormick handed him Russell's chart. He began concentrating, searching the far recesses of his mind, trying to bring to consciousness those numbers. 106-77-49, no. 106-78-59, no, that wasn't it either. Earn your reputation, Idiot Savant, he mumbled to himself. Think harder. Idiot Savant was Anderson's nickname, coined in medical school because of similarities between his ability to remember long strings of numbers and a group of severely retarded patients who, although unable to read or write, for unknown reasons were able to recall complicated lists of figures. Finally it came to him. 106-77-59. Yes, he was certain of it. 106-77-59 was Russell's unit number.

Anderson spent the following two days devising a strategy that would lead him to Russell's chart. Feigning interest in the hospital layout, he attained from Lynn James a rundown room by room, department by department and service by service. A blueprint of the hospital gradually emerged. When not questioning Ms. James on the hospital's infrastructure, Michael walked back and forth through the corridors assisted by crutches supplied by the physical therapy department. During one round trip, he spotted a flashlight lying on the threadbare couch in the nurses' lounge, accidentally left behind by a harried nurse. The room empty, he maneuvered through the doorway, seized the metal cylinder, and, finally finding a use for his oversized hospital robe, slipped the object into its pocket. The crutches definitely eased the pain, Anderson realized, but they would be too cumbersome for tonight's outing.

Twelve-ten. The graveyard shift had completed its midnight bed check. Anderson unfastened the side rails, gently let them slide down, and climbed out of bed. He put on his bathrobe, checking to make certain the flashlight was secure in its pocket, and walked to the door guided by the illumination from the night-light on the floor.

Anderson wove his way down the hospital corridor, crowded with empty carts and I.V. trays, the movement violent for a man in his condition. He decided against taking either the elevator or the main staircase. Both added unnecessary risk to an already dangerous adventure. He'd use the service stairs instead.

Quickly he opened the door to the stairwell and began descending the metal steps, worn shiny by countless footsteps.

The only light came from a bare bulb at each floor landing. On the third floor, the bulb had blown. Michael, proceeding cautiously, advanced to the next flight leading to the second floor when he remembered the flashlight. He withdrew it from his pocket and switched it on, its weak beam penetrating only a few feet. The pain in his leg made the distance between the floors seem remarkably long.

Anderson heard the door above fly open and hit the wall of the hall. He heard some steps. They were getting louder. Someone was coming down the stairs. He froze with fear, his heart jumping in its cavity. He had to move faster. One more flight to go. He had to make it. A voice called down. He ignored the command, reached the basement, opened the heavy steel door and pulling his right leg along, limped into the tunnel connecting the main hospital with the addition.

He moved along as quickly as he could. At the end of the tunnel, he reached for the handle on the door and opened it. Ahead lay a labyrinth covered in darkness. He switched on his flashlight; the beam, recharged, cast a brighter path. Suddenly a door opening somewhere in the distance, followed by hushed and hurried footsteps, then the sound of another door, then silence returned. He sighed in relief, and continued walking, his shadow appearing in front of him on the vinyl floor, growing as he walked. He came to a door on the left. If memory served him correctly, it was the doctors' on-call room. He had decided it would be safer to reach the record room from the rear rather than the front, thereby avoiding the night attendant at the desk. In his blueprint, the back of the record room opened into the doctors' lounge.

There were no sounds, and no one was in sight. There were no markings on the door. He tried the knob, the door was unlocked. He pushed open the door and stepped inside the room. The acrid smell of formaldehyde made him gag. He turned his light onto the nearby wall. The entire wall on the right had shelving from floor to ceiling, the shelves filled with various sized bottles and jars. Looking more closely, he realized the amorphous, colorless mass in the large jar closest to him was an entire human head cut neatly in half. Just behind the halved nose in the wall of the sinus was a huge mass. Anderson shuddered and tried to keep himself from glancing at the other jars. Somehow he'd made a mistake, gone the wrong direction or made a wrong turn. He wasn't in the room reserved for doctors. Rather he was in the pathology laboratory. He took a few more steps, peered through the crack between the doors up ahead. Although his vision was limited, he knew he was looking into the autopsy room.

He quickly retraced his steps, made a left out of the lab. Where did he go wrong? He tried visualizing the hospital layout. Nothing. Absolutely nothing. Where was he?

He shot his light into the room on the left. The stacks of vases and candy met his eye. The gift shop. Then he remembered, immediately adjacent to this shop was the doctors' sleeping quarters. He'd found it. Holding onto the wall for support, he hobbled to the next door, slowly opened it. There it was, two beds neatly made, waiting for a tired body to crawl between clean sheets. Michael cautiously made his way between the beds, through an alcove that led to a closed wooden door. In the center of the door in bold red letters was printed: RECORD ROOM. UNAUTHORIZED PERSONS KEEP OUT.

He gently pushed the door open, his flashlight searching through the darkness. Anderson entered the room. Row after row of manila folders. There must be thousands of charts, he thought to himself. Every hospital has their own way of filing charts so they'll be readily available when needed. It could take hours to find Russell's chart unless Anderson figured out Clarkson's filing system.

Michael walked up and down several aisles, noting unit numbers, searching for a pattern. Then he remembered he wasn't in a large metropolitan hospital. Clarkson was a small southern complex and the chances were their filing system would be simple. He eyed the chart numbers. Sure enough. The folders were numbered in sequence. In the middle of the third row on the left, he found what he had been looking for. Chart number 106-77-59, Russell's file.

As he was about to reach for the records, he heard footsteps. Carefully, Anderson edged to the wall, the shadowy figure of a man visible. He crouched down behind a large tray piled with folders to be put away. The man stopped and didn't move. Anderson guessed he was scanning the room. The man walked to the next aisle and seemed to be searching. Of course. He was searching for the lights. Anderson felt panic again take control. If he was found prowling in the record room after the incident in the nurses' station, he'd surely be sent to the psycho ward. This would be his only chance to read Russell's chart.

There was a snap of a light switch and a strong ray of light sprang from the darkened ceiling. Now Anderson could see the attendant clearly. Fortunately, the guard hadn't spotted him. There was still time, but he had to act swiftly, and with his damaged right leg that wouldn't be easy. The hospital employee walked down the far aisle, turned, and continued down the following one. Anderson peered into the space between two racks of files. The attendant was holding a pad, eyeing the shelves, removing charts and placing them under his arm. Damn! He was collecting records for tomorrow's admissions. He wouldn't be leaving the room until the job was finished. He'd eventually be in Anderson's aisle. Michael didn't have a choice, he had gotten this far, now he had to read the chart. The guard had to be silenced.

Anderson carefully lowered himself to the floor and began crawling to the front of the aisle. From this vantage point, he was able to track the guard's movements while simultaneously camouflaging his own. He crept slowly, deliberately. The attendant was now in the adjacent aisle; in five minutes, he'd be in Anderson's. He hadn't much time. Quietly he crawled to the next aisle, the guard facing the files. Then Anderson sprang up and leaped forward, ignoring the searing pain, throwing his left arm over the guard's shoulder and with his bandaged right hand digging deep into the man's rib cage. Anderson dragged the man back to the far corner of the room and spun him around, forcing him against the wall. The guard's face was a mask of terror as he tried to pull away; Anderson sunk his kneecap into the guard's groin, his fingers gripping the voice box.

Saliva poured out of the man's mouth, his chest heaving in surrender. Anderson tightened a last clamp on the guard's voice box; the air to the lungs and the head was suspended for slightly more than four seconds. The man fell limp, Anderson angled him down to the floor. He'd be out for two minutes, five tops. Fortunately, after the guard regained consciousness, he wouldn't be able to recognize his attacker. Panic clouded the mind, erased memories.

Anderson turned the unconscious body over, and whipping the belt out of the guard's trousers, he slipped it under the arms beneath the shoulder blades. He yanked it taut, looping and knotting it. Then he grabbed the guard's handkerchief and shoved it into his mouth.

Painfully Michael rose to his feet and shuffled to the middle aisle, the aisle that housed Russell's file. Reaching the row containing unit numbers 106-77-00 through 106-77-99 he scanned the column of charts and with his left hand pulled out 106-77-59. Immediately he began reading, then abruptly he stopped. Confused. This file belonged to a seventy-seven-year-old female admitted with advanced Alzheimer's. His fingers quickly raced through the pages to the final entry. Patient expired April 10. Alarmed, he flipped back through the chart, looking for her lab reports. They weren't there. The X-ray reports, also missing. Could he have made a mistake? He was certain 106-77-59 was the correct unit number. His hands trembling, he looked at the chart. The unit number on the chart matched with the one in his mind. They were identical.

The shock was as unbearable as the truth: The report he had seen at McCormick's office was not Russell's. Anderson struggled to control his rage. Somebody had gone to great lengths to deceive him. He didn't know how he would do it, but he was determined to find out who had tricked him and why.

Brian Steele stared into the full-length mirror in his suite at the Loew's L'Enfant Plaza Hotel. The sudden pains that started after being shot in the abdomen while on the front line in Da Nang and were supposed to have been relieved after he consented to intestinal surgery were plaguing him. The doctors swore they'd seen and removed the cause of the pain, shrapnel embedded in the lining of his small intestine. Why then did these bouts of incapacitating pain continue? The attacks came like clockwork, monthly. He swore it was his version of menstrual cramps.

As Steele attempted to button the trousers that went with the rest of the tuxedo he'd be wearing for tonight's black-tie dinner honoring Senator Fountain of Montana, a spasm caused him to double over. He cursed the disability, pain like hot knives stabbing through his stomach.

Steele glanced at his watch: seven-eleven. A car would be picking him up at eight. That gave him forty-nine minutes for the pain to subside. He unfastened his pants, lowered himself onto the bed and closed his eyes. Rest had a habit of relieving the spasms; tonight's dinner was too important to miss. At eight o'clock, regardless of how he felt, he'd go to the dinner even if he had to plaster on a façade. He'd been forced to do it before. If need be, he'd do it again. Damn! He hoped the pain would cooperate. Steele's circuits were overloaded: too many assignments in too short a time. Having to pretend for four hours tonight might be more than he could handle.

How differently everything turned out from what he had planned, Steele thought to himself. His youthful ambition to attend law school, eventually entering the mainstream of politics and gaining power over the masses had been destroyed forever by a single bullet fired by one of his own men in that hot, steamy jungle. His temples resonated with anger, he could smell the filth, feel the slug burst within; his dream had been shattered instantly like a glass window by a baseball. Robbed of the respectable avenue toward fame and fortune, he jumped when given the opportunity to make easy money and at the same time ruin the lives he envied, those whom fortune had blessed.

During the years his reputation solidified; he had an international following, accumulated vast sums of money, had his own Swiss bank account. But the hatred persisted, diminished only when he killed, and then only fleetingly. Always returning.

The latest attack started the night he killed Ragland. The night he crashed his car into Anderson's causing the doctor to plunge to his death, the pain had reached unbearable proportions. He thought he'd pass out while watching Anderson's car explode. Tonight's pain was equally severe. He turned to the night table and grabbed one of the pills his benefactor had given him today to combat the pain when it became unbearable.

Now was such a time. He swallowed the tablet whole, without water, and lay still, waiting for relief.

A few seconds passed. A wave of giddiness swept through his body. Steele enjoyed the feeling. Suddenly, his head throbbed, his heart began racing. He took a deep breath, then another. His chest felt as if it were closing in, as he exhaled the aroma of bitter almond.

Suddenly his muscles began twitching, slowly at first, fiber by fiber, then more rapidly, entire muscles contracting involuntarily. Steele began writhing in bed, hands clawing his face, legs kicking viciously at imaginary demons that surrounded him. His breathing became more erratic. His skin turned blue. He gasped for air, panic surging. His windpipe was closing.

Within two minutes, he was dead.

Nineteen

NOTHING WAS AS IT APPEARED, ANDERSON THOUGHT. Trust, an anathema when the effect of an action could no longer be predicted.

Sunlight bathed him in an uncomfortable warmth. The right side of his body still throbbed. He dangled his feet over the edge of the bed and flexed his swollen right ankle. A sharp twinge, bearable. He realized there was a strange, reassuring comfort about the pain, an affirmation that there still existed something he could rely on.

A dead woman's chart, used to deceive Anderson. Its impact was overpowering. If Russell didn't have Alzheimer's disease, what did he have? There still was one finding Anderson had to go on: the portable X-ray he'd taken of Russell's skull, the one that showed a definite shift of the pineal gland to the right, the X-ray that McCormick had convinced Anderson was invalid.

How readily he accepted McCormick's word that Russell had undergone four series of skull films, all of which showed the pineal gland to be in the midline, none revealing the shift that in Anderson's X-ray was apparent. He cursed himself for being so easily manipulated. A skeptic all his life, how could he have been so gullible this time?

Ruling out Alzheimer's left Anderson where he was after meeting with Stanton. Russell had a space-occupying lesion. He could only pray that whatever was ticking away inside Russell's brain wasn't yet ready to claim its victim.

He had to call Russell and warn him about McCormick. He pushed aside the breakfast tray and picked up the phone lying on the Formica table next to his bed. With his left hand, he clumsily began dialing the president's private line.

Russell had called him in, initially, because he trusted Anderson more than he did McCormick. What would he tell John, that McCormick wasn't being nonchalant and indifferent in his treatment but rather he had purposefully misdiagnosed him? No, that would only alarm the president further. He replaced the receiver down and lifted the cup of stale coffee lying on the tray, took two sips and in disgust put the cup down.

He was a doctor, not a detective. Whom could he contact? He briefly thought about Harrison before brushing aside the gargantuan chief. Paranoia, perhaps, but Anderson knew he wouldn't feel comfortable disclosing all that needed to be revealed to an agency as encompassing as the FBI.

Eric Dawson, that's who he'd phone. The man who had expressed a bona fide interest in helping Anderson before Michael knew he needed assistance.

Quickly he placed the call to the Washington paper. Every minute he lost was a minute removed from the answer and too many meant there would be no answer at all. Within three minutes, a gravelly voice picked up. "Dawson here."

"It's Mike Anderson. I need your help."

"Where are you?" Dawson replied, genuine concern in his tone.

"In Deerfield, Virginia. At Clarkson Hospital."

There was silence on the other end of the line. Finally Dawson said, "What happened? Are you okay?"

"I had an accident. It's a long story. I'll tell you everything when you get here." Anderson paused. "You will come, won't you?"

"Of course, I'll be there as soon as I can. Uh, one thing Anderson, it wasn't an accident was it?"

"No, it wasn't."

"Then do both of us a favor. Don't call anyone until I get there and we've had a chance to talk."

Anderson put the receiver down, leaned back on his pillow and stared at the bare ceiling. He didn't know if Dawson was the one to place his faith in, but after last night's marathon he was too weak to rely on himself. Anderson had to hope Dawson could be trusted. He had no other choice.

Lynn James ushered Eric Dawson into Anderson's room. "Congratulations. The staff was beginning to wonder if you had any friends." She smiled, turned on her heels, and left the room.

Michael pulled himself up in bed, pain accentuating the creases around his mouth. "Thanks for coming. Take a seat," he said, pointing to a metal straight-backed chair in the corner of the room.

Dawson complied, dragging the uncomfortable-looking chair to the side of Anderson's bed. He studied the doctor carefully. "You're quite a sight." A mixture of concern and apprehension swept across Dawson's mind: concern for Anderson, apprehension for himself. This was the first time Dawson had stepped foot inside a hospital except for assignments, since his daily treks seven years ago. For four long, agonizing months he had watched his wife waste away, her body ravaged by cancer. The feelings he thought he had buried resurfaced on seeing the various machines, oscilloscope screens, and I.V. poles in the corridor.

"How'd it happen?" Dawson asked, eyeing Anderson's bandaged leg.

Michael spoke slowly, trying to inform this man he needed to depend on. "My car was shoved off the road. Deliberately."

"You're certain it was intentional?"

Anderson shook his head, arching his eyebrows, as if recalling the impossible. "The guy behind the wheel was the same fellow who attacked me in my office." He turned, stomach churning. "Our talk convinced me that I've been a fool, denying the obvious. Trapped here with nothing to do but think and do a little snooping, I've begun to piece together events that have happened, things you've said, situations I've observed. You're right. Somebody is indeed trying to kill me, but what's emerging is far more frightening."

Dawson sat riveted to his chair. "Come to the point. What have you come up with?"

Anderson brought his folded hands to his chin, his plastic name tag scratching his skin. "First you've got to promise me nothing I tell you leaves this room."

"I can't do that. I'm a reporter. That's like asking a surgeon to operate without a scalpel."

Dawson had a point. And Anderson couldn't afford to turn away the one remaining person who might be able to help. "Okay, you win, but on one condition. Whatever articles that come out of this can't be published until I give the go-ahead."

"Why all the secrecy?"

"Hear me out and I think you'll understand why secrecy is essential."

"Agreed," Dawson reluctantly replied.

"To start with, I've a hunch there's a link between the two attempts on my life and Ragland's murder."

"Would you recognize the guy who's been after you?"

"Absolutely. I can see his face before me whenever I close my eyes. More importantly, I think I may know who he is, at least his name."

Dawson leaned forward. "Go on."

"As you've undoubtedly been aware, the FBI has been investigating Ragland's killing. Harrison called me to his office a few hours before my accident informing me his department had evidence from reliable sources that a pro, a man named Brian Steele, was responsible for the murder."

"Why did the chief of the Bureau contact you?"

"Russell asked Harrison to keep me posted on the investigation," Anderson paused. "Remember, we were all friends."

"And you believe this fellow Steele is the one who pushed your car off the road?"

"I'm not a detective, but I keep remembering your remark about coincidences. Hunt through your people's files; they must have a photo of Steele. Bring it here. If it's the same man, I'll know."

Suddenly Dawson sprang from his chair, pulled out from inside his coat pocket a copy of the morning paper and flung it at Anderson. The doctor deflected the flying object with his good arm. "What's this all about?"

"Turn to page eleven," Dawson replied. "Is that the man who's been after you?"

Anderson stirred with enthusiasm. "Damn it, yes! That's the same fellow who attacked me in my office and hurled me down the mountain! Is that Steele?"

Dawson nodded affirmatively.

"That's the lead we've needed. Harrison said that Steele is a notorious hit man. He's hired only for big game. Neither Ragland nor I qualify for that status. I am right. Something big is happening. Dawson, you've got to get to Steele. Find out who hired him."

"Forget about Steele. It's too late. He's dead."

"What?"

Dawson pointed to the article accompanying the picture. "It's all there, in black and white. He was discovered by a hotel maid late last night. He'd been dead for several hours. At the postmortem, traces of cyanide were still in his stomach. The police have pretty much ruled out suicide. They claimed things were going too well for the guy to decide to bump himself off."

"Steele murdered!" Anderson screamed.

"That's what the MPD believe. They're working on the assumption whoever hired him felt he had outlived his usefulness."

Another unexpected blow. Anderson's head sank into the pillow, his mind whirling.

"That's too bad. Your hunches were right, only they came too late to do us any good," Dawson replied softly.

"Wait a minute," Anderson sat bolt upright in his bed. "Sometimes the most relevant evidence is right in front of us, and we don't see it. We dig so hard for details, we miss the obvious, the way it can provoke a thought, give rise to an image, prod a connection. I don't agree with you. We're not at all too late."

"You've lost me."

"Russell's not been acting like himself for months. You know that. What you don't know is he asked me to examine him. That meant working through his physician, Dr. Art McCormick. I think I've finally figured out a large chunk of the puzzle."

"Then fill me in on it."

"I better backtrack a bit. It was obvious after examining Russell that his memory was impaired. I called McCormick, alerting him to my findings. From that moment on, the bastard has been feeding me wild stories, and I've believed them.

Every last one of them. Delays in evaluating Russell kept popping up. Nothing was being done. I'm so absorbed with my own problems I accept McCormick's reasons. Finally he shows me Russell's hospital chart. I accept the results of the work-up. Alzheimer's disease. A horrible way to go, but findings are findings." Anderson smashed his right fist into the mattress, wincing from the pain. "When Russell told me he never was hospitalized, what did I think? Poor guy, consistent with his memory loss. My one concern: How rapidly was his memory slipping? Then my car accident. I land up here and inadvertently discover this was the same place Russell was supposedly evaluated in. Making like James Bond, I get his record, find out it's not his. That I've been duped. That McCormick conned me. That Russell most likely doesn't have Alzheimer's disease after all."

"Why would McCormick want to deceive you?"

"I think it goes far deeper than that. McCormick is going all out to prevent me from helping the president. Ragland was furious at the indifference McCormick displayed in Russell's deteriorating condition. Then Ragland is found murdered. Dawson, I'm convinced McCormick hired Steele to kill Ragland and to get rid of me. You've got to find out what McCormick is up to. What can be so important that he's purposefully misdiagnosing the president and at the same time having Ragland and me disposed of?"

Dawson leaned back in his chair, beads of sweat forming on his forehead. "Do you realize what you're saying?"

"You bet I do! It's taken a long time to pull things together, but Steele's murder accomplished that. There is a conspiracy going on, a conspiracy against the president of the United States. A conspiracy that involves McCormick. You've got to find out what it's all about, what role McCormick is playing in it, and who else is involved."

Anderson collapsed onto his pillow. "Right now, I'm obviously not in any condition to get out of here and help you. It's your ball game."

"You were serious when you said this story could be a big one. Relax. I'll take care of things from here on in. Whatever McCormick's up to, I'll find out." Dawson got up to leave. "I'm going to pay our friend an unexpected visit."

He stopped in the doorway. "I've agreed to abide by your condition. I won't write this up without your permission. Now I've got a condition you must live with. I'm going to write an article for tomorrow's paper, have it run front page and in all editions. I want everybody to read it. It's going to be about your fatal car crash."

"What!" Anderson barked.

"You heard me. By this time tomorrow everybody in Washington will think you're dead. Killed in a tragic automobile accident."

"You're crazy!"

"My mental state isn't the issue, getting to the bottom of this conspiracy and your safety are. With McCormick believing he's successfully gotten rid of you, his guard will be down, my chances for tripping him up, much greater."

"What about Russell? Have you considered the effect this news coming so soon after Ragland's death will have on him?"

Dawson's voice rose. "That's a luxury we can't concern ourselves with."

Anderson became alarmed. "What about the president's medical condition? He needs my help, and urgently."

"I've no counterargument. You might be right. But everything can't be done at once. You called on me, now trust me. I know what I'm doing."

Dr. Wheeler finished removing Anderson's sutures and disappeared down the hall when the telephone rang, the bell vibrating through Michael's hand, the shrill sound unnerving. It must be Dawson. He's gotten to McCormick. Anderson's spirits were buoyed by the thought. Two days had passed since their conversation. Anderson eagerly raised the receiver to his ear. "Hello."

"Michael, is that you?"

Anderson felt a sinking sensation in the pit of his stomach. The voice at the other end of the line wasn't Dawson's.

"Hello, Michael?"

The voice sounded strained, frantic. It was a female's voice. He recognized the caller. "Kate!" Anderson replied. "How in God's name did you find me?"

"It really is you. I was beginning to lose hope."

"You didn't answer me. How did you know I was here?" Anderson asked, his anxiety mounting. If Kate was able to locate him, McCormick would be able to. Obviously, Dawson's plan hadn't worked.

"I'm a Scot remember? We're a determined people. When I didn't hear from you, I tried calling your home. I was going to apologize for the way I've been carrying on, but there was no answer. After several more attempts, I gave up and called your service. They were as puzzled as I was." She paused. "It's so good to talk to you. Are you all right?"

"Yes, I'm okay, had some bumps and bruises but they're practically healed," Anderson replied, a warm feeling settling over him. "How'd you find me?"

"I felt at a complete loss. Then I remembered Margaret, the girl who cleans your office. When my regular housekeeper is unavailable, I've occasionally asked Margaret to help me out. She's always come through. I called her, told her I was afraid something had happened to you and asked if she'd let me into your office so I could rummage through your desk. I know you have a habit of jotting down social and personal things in the margins of your appointment book. Sure enough, I was right.

There, written in your unique scrawl was a phone number with the area code 202. I knew 202 meant Washington. I called the number and was connected with the Lee Hotel. I explained my predicament to the manager. He was understanding and quite helpful, telling me that you had been a guest at the hotel, but had apparently been in some kind of car accident. He didn't know the details, but a man picked up your belongings and paid your bill, saying you were currently in a hospital and wouldn't be returning to the hotel. He slipped the manager a hundred dollar bill on the promise he'd delete your name from the hotel's log."

That must have been Dawson, Anderson thought, feeling more secure with the realization that the reporter was indeed clever. "How did you get the manager to reveal this information?"

"Like I told you, I'm Scottish. Do you want to hear the rest?"

"Do you want to tell me?" Anderson quipped.

"Absolutely. I want you to know how persistent I can be when I finally wake up. I realized I might have blown everything by my petty insecurities and my ridiculous need for attention. I needed to find you, to tell you how wrong I had been to push things. Anyway, you've been acting tense and irritable lately, and I remembered your tonic when you felt this way had always been to get into your car and drive into the country. Since you were in Washington, I figured you probably were driving through either Maryland or Virginia when the accident occurred. I went to the public library, the reference librarian handed me a book that listed all hospitals in the country by state, and maps of Virginia and Maryland. I jotted down the seventy-five hospitals that fell within a one-hundred-mile radius of Washington. You'll never believe this, but Clarkson is the fifty-seventh one I've called."

Michael was speechless, stunned by the depth of caring Kate's efforts symbolized.

"I don't want to pry, so tell me to shut up if you wish, but you're such a careful driver. How'd it happen?"

"It wasn't an accident. The same man who attacked me in my office ran me off the road," Anderson replied, shocked at the spontaneity of his remark and the complete absence of anger at being questioned. "One of the nurses told me I owe my life to an off-duty cop who happened to be driving by at the time."

"Mike, what have you gotten involved with? Why is someone trying to kill you?" Kate asked, frightened.

"I don't know yet. But I hope I'll find the answer within a few days. You've heard of Eric Dawson, haven't you?"

"The reporter from the Washington paper?"

"That's him. I'm counting on Dawson to solve this mess I'm in. Part of his plan involves having it appear that I was killed in the accident. So you'll likely come across an article, maybe even an obituary. Don't panic. Believe me, I'm alive. If you need reassurance, call Dawson. You must promise not to contact me again. I'll call you when I'm out of the hospital and back in New York. It should be sometime next week. Do I have your word?"

"Michael, I don't understand what's going on, but if calling you is only going to jeopardize your life further, of course I'll do as you ask."

"And Kate, I realize I haven't been fair to you. After this nightmare is over, I'm really going to try."

Anderson disconnected the line with his index finger. He couldn't believe he'd said that to Kate and, furthermore, that he meant it.

The sky was overcast, the air heavy and oppressive. A steady drizzle threatened to become a downpour. The crowds in front of the gate were quiet after a day filled with angry protests from the urban unemployed who had flocked to the nation's capitol to vent their outrage at the sudden policy shift that threatened to rob them of their dignity.

McCormick looked away from the sullen faces of those remaining and walked towards Russell, seated on a couch near the fireplace. Peg was on a chair beside him. The mood in the Oval Office was bleak, the melancholia pronounced.

"Mr. President," McCormick began, positioning himself on the couch next to Russell. "There's nothing I can say to ease your sorrow. You've suffered a tragic loss in Anderson's death. But, Mr. President, we both know you have a mission to accomplish. You've got to pull yourself together. Think of the summit. Your lifelong dream. Use your energies to plan your strategy. It will ease your loss."

Russell looked directly into McCormick's penetrating, deep blue eyes. He thought he noticed something eerily menacing in them, something he'd never seen before. Quickly he suppressed the notion. Without Ragland and Anderson, he needed McCormick now more than ever.

Peg relaxed in her chair, the confidence in her lover's voice was contagious.

The doctor reached into his medical satchel, dug out a syringe equipped with a one-millimeter needle, and with his free hand grabbed a small vial of Nembutal, drew one cc into the plastic container and deftly plunged it into Russell's waiting right arm. Slowly the barbiturate entered the president's bloodstream. "Now you'll be able to get some much needed rest. I'll come by in the morning. Remember, Mr. President, I'm with you all the way. You're going to get to that summit and do one hell of a job. Count on me. I won't let you down."

Twenty

A TREMENDOUS AMOUNT OF INGENUITY, THAT'S WHAT it had taken, Dawson proudly thought, congratulating himself as he stepped from his car and began the short walk to McCormick's Georgetown office.

He had had to orchestrate this afternoon's meeting with utmost care, disguising its true intent lest McCormick's suspicions be aroused. An investigative reporter arriving at a doctor's doorstep, unannounced and uninvited, would hardly have succeeded.

Lunch at Le Lion d'Or three days ago with Henry Jackson had started a chain reaction that Dawson hoped would lead an unsuspecting doctor to reveal more than he bargained for.

Dawson carefully fed the ambitious New York reporter enough to whet his appetite without disclosing anything of significance. At the same time he stroked Jackson's ego by alluding to his being at an impasse in his attempt to find out why Russell was dodging the press. A dead end that only Jackson, because of his excellent rapport with Vice-President Kingsley and Cullie Hamilton could help him surmount. Dawson promised that he would disclose all he learned to his colleague.

Tasting victory, Jackson arranged for Dawson to meet

Kingsley the next morning and Hamilton the following afternoon. With Kingsley, Dawson touched briefly on the vice-president's views and on his accomplishments while in office. After finishing, Dawson confided in Kingsley that he'd been having a problem, a medical problem, that it had something to do with his blood pressure. He'd lost confidence in his internist, had heard great things about President Russell's physician, knew McCormick occasionally took on private patients but only on personal recommendations. Dawson asked if it would be too much of an inconvenience for the vice-president to call McCormick and alert him to his predicament. In return, Dawson promised a spread in his column dealing with Kingsley's role in the present administration. Kingsley jumped at the offer.

Cullie Hamilton was more cunning and harder to cajole, but in the end the results were the same: a pledge to give the Senate majority leader ample coverage in his column in return for a phone call setting up an appointment with Art McCormick to evaluate a friend of his, Eric Dawson, for hypertension.

If Dawson was concerned enough to have two heavyweights get him a second opinion, he realized he had to know something about his presumed problem. Ninety minutes at Johns Hopkins spent talking to cardiologists and reading up on the ideology and treatment of high blood pressure proved sufficient.

Dawson strolled past a row of townhouses, bordered by gardens consisting of circles of bursting marigolds before coming to 18 Hathaway. A doorman stood in front of the five-floor, solid structure of heavy white stone that once housed Washington's genteel set but now served as professional offices. The rotund man in brown opened the heavy glass door. "Pardon, sir," said the man. "Who are you coming to see?"

"Dr. McCormick."

"Take the elevator to the second floor. The receptionist will assist you."

The receptionist referred to was a middle-aged woman with silver-white close-cropped hair and tortoiseshell glasses. "Can I help you?" she asked courteously.

"I've an appointment with Dr. McCormick at two."

The woman glanced at the wall clock. "It's only one-thirty, take a seat. The doctor isn't in yet. I'm sure you're familiar with these." She handed him a form. "Please fill in your name, address, phone number, insurance coverage, if any, and past medical history."

Dawson sat down in an imitation Chippendale chair and began filling out the form, pleased at how everything so far had gone as planned. Hamilton's complaining at length about McCormick's irritating habit of arriving late for appointments gave Dawson the idea to come earlier than expected this afternoon. He wanted to be left alone, to have time to look around McCormick's office. He had no doubt the woman at the desk was well acquainted with McCormick's tardiness and that if he played his cards right, he'd shortly win her sympathies and she'd let him wait in the doctor's office, especially if he began complaining of a severe headache, a frequent symptom in patients suffering from hypertension.

At fifteen-minute intervals, Dawson went through his routine, asking when McCormick could be expected and mentioning he wasn't feeling well.

Finally, at a quarter to three, she apologized for McCormick's delayed arrival and suggested Dawson lie down and rest in the doctor's office. Dawson cheerfully consented.

The room was paneled and tastefully furnished, a heavy mahogany desk in front of a bay window, two leather armchairs next to one another and across from them a couch flanked by antique tables. Up-to-date magazines were neatly arranged on the table. Dawson glanced at the book-lined walls, biographies of famous men predominating, men of strong will, determination, and rigidity. Figures such as Alexander the Great, Bismarck, Churchill, Franklin Delano Roosevelt, Einstein, and Hitler. An odd choice of books for a medical office, he thought, yet on further scrutiny everything about the room reflected the personality characteristics McCormick's colleagues at Walter Reed had described. An austere, aloof, fastidious individual, extremely conscientious and inflexible, with an old-world European aura about him. Not one physician he spoke to considered McCormick a friend; several believed he was a loner, without any close relationships. Dawson learned from another internist at the hospital that McCormick originally came from somewhere in the Midwest and was presently divorced. All the doctors Dawson met joked about McCormick's famous lists. It seemed the doctor had an inordinate fear of forgetting and therefore making mistakes. To compensate he carried index cards wherever he went, constantly jotting down things that needed his attention and checking them off when they were completed.

The doctor might be viewed as a benign eccentric to his colleagues, but Anderson had convinced Dawson otherwise, that McCormick was malignant and that it was up to Dawson to find out what he was up to and do so at once.

Dawson eyed his watch: 2:55 P.M. If he was right, that gave him twenty minutes before McCormick would arrive at the office. He reached into his trouser pocket and pulled out a large green and white capsule, placed it near the back of his throat and quickly swallowed it. He had used Dexedrine in the past when he had deadlines to meet that necessitated staying alert for long stretches of time. The pill was the same; its purpose now different. He needed the increase in blood pressure the amphetamine produced.

Within seven minutes the rush started, his face became flushed, his heartbeat more forceful, his pulse resonated in his temples.

Dawson rapidly made his way to the file cabinet. Nothing unusual there. Just patient's charts. Nothing on Russell. He was looking for something, anything that would shed light on what McCormick was up to.

Many years spent as a reporter had taught Dawson to look for inconsistencies in those he was investigating, contrary aspects of their personalities that inevitably led to their downfall. With McCormick, he believed it was the contradiction between his compulsive nature and his inability to be punctual. Most compulsive people avoid being late. They make it a point to come to appointments either on time or even early. They can't handle the anxiety if they don't.

No wonder McCormick insisted on getting down on paper everything that had to be done, Dawson thought. These opposing traits greatly increased McCormick's chances of slipping up. Dawson hoped the mistake this time would be a big one.

He moved to the doctor's desk and continued his search. Drug samples, pens, note pads, assorted pencils. In disgust he slammed the top drawer shut and was about to turn away when he noticed a small white object protruding from under the brown blotter, its position dislodged by the impact.

He immediately pushed the blotter aside; a three by five index card emerged. Dawson quickly picked up the card. He couldn't believe his eyes. Before him was what he had been looking for, evidence to substantiate Anderson's claim: an itemized list of important matters that had to be taken care of along with a check mark next to each detail that had been successfully completed. He began reading.

Items on Agenda

1. Treating of Russell without change, daily reassurances
2. Ragland √
3. Anderson √
4. Steele √
5. Impress committee members, especially Hamilton
6. All systems go

Dawson heard noise outside the door. It was McCormick talking to the receptionist. Quickly he shoved the index card into his pants pocket, replaced the blotter in its correct position, and tried to regain his composure. He had found what he had come for. Now he had to hope the Dexedrine had sufficiently elevated his blood pressure so that McCormick would become concerned. Otherwise the doctor's suspicious nature would be unnecessarily aroused. He raced to the couch and took a deep breath as a broad-shouldered man in a tailor-made navy blue suit entered. The well-fitting clothes accentuated the doctor's muscular physique. He walked around the desk, straightening the blotter, and nodded toward the leather armchair in front of the desk. "Sorry for the delay. Do sit down."

Dawson got up and moved to the chair.

"I've read some of your work. Very impressive. Please roll up your sleeve."

McCormick took the sphygmomanometer out of his medical bag, came around the desk and wrapped the cuff around Dawson's right arm, inflating the tubing and then slowly opening the valve releasing the air. "It's 170/110." McCormick ran his thick fingers through his hair. "That's quite high. What does it usually run?"

Dawson's anxiety lessened, McCormick appeared genuinely concerned about the reading. The Dexedrine had worked. "I'm not sure. That's one of the reasons I asked Kingsley and Hamilton if they wouldn't mind doing me a favor and asking you to see me. The internist I've been seeing shrugs me off whenever I've asked. He just says it's a little high."

"That's outrageous! It's your body. You should know. What's his name?"

"If you wouldn't mind, I'd rather not say. He's been treating members of my family for years. He's a good guy. I don't want his reputation to suffer. I just want to feel better."

McCormick lifted his eyebrows. "Have you been having any symptoms?"

"Headaches. I have one right now." Dawson turned to face the door. "That's why your receptionist let me wait in here."

"Any others?"

"Occasionally I get light-headed."

McCormick repeated the procedure. "175/110. In my experience, two similar readings separated by a few minutes are a good indicator of your actual blood pressure." He removed the cuff. "I want you to have a hypertensive work-up. I'll arrange for it to be done."

Dawson interrupted. "No, that won't be necessary. You've been more than kind. I know you're a busy man. I only wanted confirmation. You've given me that. Just refer me to a good cardiologist. I'll set things up myself."

McCormick leaned forward in his chair. "Whatever you say. Give Frank Emerling a call. He's chief of cardiology at Georgetown. Tell him I referred you."

McCormick stood in front of his bookcase, removed the volume on Napoleon, scanned it briefly and carried it to his desk. He sat down and reached into the lower desk drawer, pulled out two index cards and began reading his book, stopping every few pages to jot down some information on one of the cards.

Suddenly he picked his head up, his eyes falling on the

blotter. He wanted to write one of Napoleon's quotations on the index card that he kept under the blotter. The piece of paper that was too important to risk carrying around. He searched blindly with his fingers. Something was wrong. He couldn't find it. Where was it? Frantically, he threw aside the leather blotter. It wasn't there. The card was missing. He knew it had been there this morning when he checked off Steele's name. Nobody had been in the office since then. Nobody . . . except Dawson.

McCormick got out of his chair, his eyes glazed, his body trembling. "Damn Dawson! He could ruin everything!"

The telephone rang. It had to be Dawson. Kate had promised not to call, no one else knew he was there. Anderson picked up the phone.

"Score one for me! Mike, we hit the jackpot!" Dawson said, his voice euphoric.

Anderson, seated on the vinyl chair next to his hospital bed, swallowed hard. "What'd you find?"

"Your theory about McCormick was right on target. I finagled some time alone in his office this afternoon and found a card listing six points. The first had something to do with Russell's medical problem, the second, Ragland's name, the third, yours, and the fourth, Steele's. The three names were checked off. I'm not clear about the meaning of the fifth and sixth points as yet but there's no doubt about it, there is a conspiracy going on."

"What's the next step?" Anderson asked.

"Stay where you are. The story about your accident ran in yesterday's paper. McCormick is convinced you're dead. I'm going to poke around. Cullie Hamilton's name was on the card. I'm going to drop in on him. I don't know what's going on yet, but I'll find out." Dawson paused. "Mike, hold on will you? My doorbell just rang. It's probably my editor. He said he might stop by for a drink. I'll be right back."

Anderson held the phone to his ear and with his other hand picked up a succulent peach Lynn James had picked especially for him. He took a large bite, savoring its sweet taste, then another, then another. What was taking Dawson so long to answer the door?

Suddenly he heard a click followed by a dial tone. Damn it! What a time to be disconnected. He quickly dialed the operator and explained the situation to her. "One minute, please, I'll ring it for you. I'm sorry, sir. The party isn't answering."

"That's impossible! Operator, try again."

She dialed once more. Again, no response. Anderson was surprised, his face reflecting his astonishment. Twenty-five minutes passed. He tried again. Busy. Strange, Anderson thought, that Dawson didn't call right back. Then he remembered Eric mentioning that he wanted to get in touch with Cullie Hamilton and concluded he must have decided to call him instead. He shrugged his shoulders and continued reading the current issue of the *Smithsonian*.

Fifty minutes later, the line was still busy. He looked at his watch: ten-fifty-five. The hospital switchboard closed at eleven. He hoped Dawson's ninety-minute talk with Hamilton was reaping rewards. Anderson tossed his magazine onto the floor, annoyed he'd have to wait until morning to finish his conversation with Eric.

Anderson crushed out the cigarette in the ashtray on the bedside table. It was five minutes to seven. He'd been up most of the night, unable to sleep, reading the *Potomac Quarterly* waiting for the switchboard to reopen.

He stared at the second hand as it circled the dial. Five rotations and he'd be able to use the phone. Coping with the tension of waiting, a practice he was normally superb at, was causing him pain, actual physical pain in his stomach. At last, eight o'clock. Dawson would be at work. Anderson breathed deeply, grabbed the phone and dialed Dawson's private line at the paper. After four rings, the phone was picked up. A man answered. A man with a different voice. Where was Dawson? His colleague didn't know. He had been expected a half hour ago.

Anderson's heart skipped a beat. He quickly dialed Dawson's home. The line was still busy. Impatience was replaced by apprehension. He dialed the operator. "Could you please ring area code (301) 249-9923? I've been trying for hours. I keep getting a busy signal," he said masking his concern.

The reply came forty seconds later. "That line is busy."

"That's impossible! Is there something the matter with the line?"

"One minute please. I'll check further."

Anderson waited.

The operator broke the silence. "There's nothing the matter with the line. There's no one on it. The phone's off the hook."

Anderson slammed the phone down, his mind flashing back to the ringing of Dawson's doorbell that had interrupted their talk. Whoever was at the door held the answer.

A sense of helplessness overcame him, a feeling that would continue as long as he remained in the hospital. He had to get out of Clarkson, out of Deerfield, to Annapolis, to Dawson.

He rang for the floor nurse. In a few minutes Lynn James appeared in the doorway. "What's up?"

"I've got to get out of here. Now. Immediately."

"Hold on. What's this all about?"

"I don't have time to explain. Just get me out of here."

"I can't. Dr. Wheeler isn't in. He's the only one who can give the order."

"Then get a hold of him and fast! Either he agrees to discharge me, or I'll sign out. I'm serious."

"Okay, I'll try to locate him."

"No!" Anderson said pointing to the phone. "Call here."

Lynn reached Wheeler at home. His answer was clear from the expression on her face.

"Get me my things. I'm signing out," Anderson said.

The drive to Annapolis took three hours. Finding a car rental agency in the Virginian Hills was no easy matter and then buying new clothes to replace the ripped. blood-soaked ones he had worn at the time of the accident ate up another twenty-five minutes. His weakness and dizziness didn't help either. At last he turned into a long circular driveway, the white post-and-rail fence demarcating the journalist's property. The large, modern colonial-style house was set far back from the road. The grounds were cleared in the front, but on the sides thick, tall trees shot up randomly around the lawn.

Anderson parked his Hertz rental, tapping it on the hood for doing a better job than its predecessor, noticed Dawson's car in the opened garage, and walked to the front door. He pressed on the bell, the chimes reverberating on the other side of the entrance. He waited a moment before pressing again. No response. He peered through the small window adjacent to the door. Nobody was approaching. He tried the doorknob. Much to his surprise, the door wasn't locked. It flew open. Anderson stepped inside, stood briefly in the foyer, eyed the two Chinese porcelain vases and walked into the immaculate living room.

The air was hot, stale, the windows shut. Why wasn't the air conditioning on? "Dawson? Dawson, where are you?" Anderson called.

The doctor's body tensed. He walked quickly into the dining room. Nobody. Nothing. He was ready to turn and walk to the den when he saw a small stain on the beige carpet. He knelt down, flinching, his right leg still painful. He touched the discolored area. It was dry. He leaned his nose over the spot. It had a distinctive smell. There was no longer any doubt in his mind. The pigment was dried blood. He eyed the rest of the carpet. His stomach sank as he recognized several other drops of blood. He slowly rose from his crouched position and followed the red marks, becoming increasingly fearful of what he'd find at the end of the trail.

He swallowed hard and took a deep breath, then another. He smelt something. There was something peculiarly familiar about the odor. He continued walking, following the ever increasing number of red stains, the smell intensifying. Finally he reached a small hallway. He looked up. Ahead loomed the kitchen.

Anderson knew it was useless, but once again he called out for the reporter, for the one man who was sharing his horror.

Silence.

He entered the kitchen. A wave of nausea swept over him. He recognized the smell, that horrible stench. It was the odor of decaying flesh. Halfway inside the room he stopped. Lying on the floor in a pool of blood, his right hand tightly grasping the telephone, was Dawson. His head a mass of dark red. No wonder Dawson's line was busy, Anderson thought. After being shot, he must have gotten to the kitchen and tried calling me. Anderson braced his shaking body against the refrigerator. Dawson had gotten too close. He hadn't been as fortunate as Anderson. He didn't survive.

He held his breath, bent down and began searching Dawson, looking for the index card Eric had mentioned on the phone, the piece of paper that led to Dawson's murderer. It would give Anderson what he needed, leads to follow. He turned Dawson over, and went through his pockets, then ripped his shirt off, then his pants, finally taking off his socks and shoes, plowing through everything, overlooking nothing. That card. Where was that card?

Finally he realized the hunt was in vain and slowly lifted himself up from the vinyl floor.

McCormick must have discovered the index card was missing, suspected Dawson, driven here, killed him, and retrieved the damaging evidence. No other explanation was possible, Anderson thought, as he slammed the front door behind him. The one man he had counted on was dead. The maze was more frightening than ever because now he had to solve it alone.

Twenty-one

GETTING BACK TO MANHATTAN WAS THE TONIC ANDERson needed, the distance from Washington allowing perspective to slowly emerge. Twenty-four hours by himself, without interruptions, time spent sifting through, dissecting and analyzing the harrowing events of the past several weeks, events that culminated with Dawson's death. The reporter had linked McCormick not only to the destructive manner in which he was treating the president's critical medical problem, but with the attempt on Anderson's life as well.

McCormick's intentions were unknown. Those in a position to ferret them out, dead. McCormick was now Anderson's sole source of information; it remained unclear how he'd proceed. He wanted to call Russell, to let him know he was alive, that McCormick was spearheading a conspiracy. Then he remembered Dawson's admonition, and reluctantly agreed the murdered newspaper man was right. He'd be calling for his own sake, not for the president's. The risks were too great. Anderson first had to find concrete evidence to substantiate his belief. Then he'd tell Russell.

Michael wandered into the living room, to the built-in wall unit, opened the cabinet doors and turned on the stereo. Light, romantic music floated from the speakers, covering his bewilderment. Anderson needed a new avenue to explore, a new direction to turn. He picked up the morning edition of the *Times* lying on the coffee table, sat down on the leather couch and began reading. On page four, tucked in alongside a story about acid rain, was a small headline followed by a paragraph of no more than one hundred and fifty words that supplied Anderson with the path he was searching for.

The article stated that Stan Wilkinson, the undersecretary of state, had just returned from a goodwill tour of developing third world countries.

Last year while addressing the Bar Association's annual convention at the Waldorf, Wilkinson was suddenly seized by severe abdominal pain. He was taken to New York Hospital. Russell alerted Anderson who rushed to the emergency room. The diagnosis: acute duodenal ulcer. It took several days of intensive treatment before Wilkinson's condition stabilized. After discharge, Wilkinson discovered Anderson was to have left for a week's vacation in the Caribbean, a vacation aborted because of the undersecretary's hospitalization. Deeply grateful, Wilkinson insisted Anderson contact him if he ever needed assistance.

This was the time; Wilkinson the ideal choice. The undersecretary of state moved in the highest governmental circles and could easily gain access to McCormick's confidential file, the secret dossier that the CIA and the FBI maintained on all important presidential appointees. Anderson was certain McCormick's file containing everything about the doctor's background would include specific information that at the time he was appointed Russell's personal physician was not thought important. But to Anderson it might appear significant now.

The fact that Wilkinson had only returned yesterday from twenty days in Africa was an added bonus. He probably wouldn't have heard about Anderson's accident and presumed death. Anderson could therefore contact him secure in the knowledge his secret would remain intact.

The more he thought of calling Wilkinson, the more the idea appealed to him. He felt a sense of hope returning as he dialed the State Department.

The black telephone rang on Stan Wilkinson's desk, its bell quiet. The career diplomat lurched for the phone, his eyes bloodshot from lack of sleep, his mind still disoriented from jet lag.

Wilkinson braced himself against the desk as he picked up the phone. "Yes?"

"It's Mike Anderson. How's the ulcer?"

"It was fine until I overdid it while in Africa. I really pigged out, now I'm paying the price. What can I do for you?"

"I thought I'd collect my IOU."

"Don't tell me your passport expired!"

"No, what I'm about to ask you to do has nothing to do with vacation plans. It's far more important than that."

Wilkinson was taken aback by the seriousness of the doctor's voice. "What's up?"

"You know Art McCormick, don't you?"

"Certainly. A good man. We golf together."

Anderson, surprised, replied, "I had no idea you two were friends."

"I wouldn't go that far. I don't mean to be rude, but my ulcer's acting up and I'm exhausted, so come to the point."

"I want you to go through McCormick's file and let me know everything you can about the man, everything from his personal habits to who he voted for in last year's election."

"Why?"

"Stan, you owe me a favor. Please do what I've asked. I'd rather not answer your question, at least not until you've gotten the information I'm looking for."

"Which is what?"

"I don't know . . . as yet. Please, just do it. And Stan, one more favor. Don't tell Russell or McCormick about our conversation."

"Okay. Okay, but I still think you're nuts."

Anderson replied, "I'll be in Washington the day after tomorrow. Let's get together for dinner. Say at six at the Lancelot in Crystal City."

"The Lancelot! You are out of your mind! Washington might not be New York City, but we do have our share of excellent hotels and restaurants."

"Please, Stan. You promised. No questions asked. Just go through McCormick's file with a fine-tooth comb."

"You're wasting your time, but I owe you. I'll see you at six, in Crystal City, at the Lancelot," Wilkinson answered, shaking his head in disbelief.

Kate was on her love seat, in her nightgown, her knees drawn up under her, reading *Architectural Digest* when the doorbell rang. She jumped up and opened the door. "Mike! Good God, I don't believe it's you! Why didn't you warn me? I must be a mess."

"Aren't you going to invite me in?"

Still stunned, Kate replied, "Of course. How'd you get past the doorman?"

Michael took out his billfold. "Money talks. It even buys surprises." He swept back the wisps of hair which fell over the near side of her face. She didn't move as he tilted her face so he could see her eyes.

There is something different about him, Kate thought. What it was she didn't know.

"I kept my word. Just remember that," Anderson said.

She flung both her arms around his neck. "I'm so happy to see you! What a relief. You seem in one piece. Why all the secrecy and what was that nonsense about your obituary?"

"Forget it. I'll tell you later. How'd you like to see my art work?"

She laughed as Michael took off his trousers. "A seamstress could have sewn a straighter line."

Anderson smiled, and then joined her in laughter. Laughter was not inconsequential. Her laugh especially. It lessened the pressure.

Michael walked with Kate through the elegant living room, guided her to her bedroom, and then, putting both his arms under her slim body, carried her over to her bed.

Afterwards, they lay together, unwilling after being so long apart to drift into sleep. Anderson's usual aloofness seemed to have melted away, replaced by a mood of tenderness and warmth. Kate liked the change, the absence of the usual barrier, but she wasn't going to let herself get carried away and press too hard, too fast. She'd learned her lesson. From here on, she'd take one step at a time.

"Can you tell me what's happening?" Kate asked, her head leaning on Michael's chest.

"I'd like to," he replied, turning and looking directly into her eyes, his facial muscles tightening, "but you're better off not knowing what's going on."

"Michael, tonight was the first time I ever felt we made love. That we were truly intimate. Sharing your problems would only bring us closer. Trust me enough to unburden yourself."

Anderson hesitated briefly before replying, "Somebody is trying to kill me. I don't want you hurt. It's as simple as that."

"Good God!" Kate said, her face suddenly filled with fear as the memory of seeing Michael's bruised body after he was attacked in his office surfaced. "Then it wasn't a car accident."

"No."

"Were you run off the road by the same man who was in your office that night?"

"Yes."

"Then he's still after you?"

"No, he's been killed."

"Then it's all over."

"No, there's more to it than that." Michael paused before continuing. "Kate, I've told you more than I should, more than is safe for you to know. Believe me, the less you know about this the better."

"Michael, I love you. I'm scared for you." She hugged him, tears running down her cheeks.

Those words. Anderson waited to see how his body would react, waiting for the abdominal pain that inevitably followed. It didn't come. Instead a warm glow developed. "I'll be all right."

Anderson thought it best to reassure Kate. "The police have been very helpful. They're convinced they know what's going on. They expect very shortly to have everything solved."

"I don't understand. It's all so confusing."

"I know, but once this is over I'll tell you everything." Anderson climbed out of bed and grabbed his trousers.

"Do you have to leave?"

"Yes. I didn't think it was smart to come in the first place, but"—he paused—"I promised and . . . I meant it when I said I'm going to try and make this work. Remember, Dawson believes it's best for the killer to think he succeeded, so if anyone asks—"

Kate interrupted, "Don't worry. Just promise me you'll be careful."

The morning sun splashed into the room as Anderson put down the telephone after speaking to Kate. She agreed to call Jeff Leeds and ask him to continue covering Michael's practice for at least another week. Anderson knew Leeds well. He had been one of his residents, and would gladly consent to cover without questioning why.

That left Michael with a clear calendar and his dinner with Wilkinson still thirty-four hours away, ample time to take the shuttle to Boston and visit Dick Landey.

Landey, an old friend, had helped him through a particularly difficult period twenty-five years ago. Anderson's medical studies had been severely affected by ever-increasing problems with his mother. Dr. Landey had succeeded in getting Anderson back on course.

Michael needed Landey's help again. This time another person was standing in his way, blocking him. The psychiatrist had taught him how to deal effectively with his mother. Now Anderson hoped he'd show him a way to handle McCormick.

August over, Labor Day approaching, Landey would be back from his annual pilgrimage to the Cape. But not yet back to work. It would be a good time for him to see Michael.

The thin, balding man with a white stubble of a beard wearing a green surgical scrub suit greeted Anderson warmly on his arrival. "Michael, it's good to see you," Landey said, patting his friend and former patient on the back. "I know you want to talk. I do my best thinking while jogging."

"That's not a good idea. I'm recovering from an accident and can just about walk."

"Then you've never seen me run. Believe me, you'll have no trouble keeping pace," Landey replied as he led Anderson into his paneled den and handed him a brown scrub suit. "Here, put this on. I borrowed an extra one from Mass. General for just such an occasion."

Michael undressed and slipped the surgical uniform on. His trust total, he began talking, the words flowing, every detail revealed, all events related. When Anderson had finished, Landey stood silently, scratching his whiskers and then replied, "Come on. I see we have lots to discuss."

The two men pushed through the front door of the brownstone and out onto Commonwealth Avenue. Anderson's legs, initially stiff, gradually developed fluidity. Landey was right. He jogged so slowly anyone could keep up with him. Michael took a deep breath, enjoying the cooler New England air.

They jogged to Storrow Drive and turned onto the tamarack-lined path paralleling the river, passing oarsmen sculling the Charles, people scattered along the grassy banks reading, sketching, or just sunbathing. Dogs pulling their masters along, roller skaters noisily passing in both directions. A barefoot blonde wearing jeans sent a Frisbee spinning toward her boyfriend; it curved and landed at Landey's feet. The psychiatrist bent down, scooped up the spherical object and flipped it back to the girl. "Now, how about our getting back to you!"

Anderson began, "You know what bothers me the most? It's that I feel so stupid. I can't believe it took me this long to connect McCormick with all that's been going on. I can't understand how I misjudged him so badly."

"Don't be so hard on yourself. I probably would have been taken in by him also."

"Bullshit! I've seen you at work. Five minutes and you come up with a personality profile that's right on target."

"Ah, Mike, that's because of my professional detachment and objectivity. But I only use those qualities while I'm evaluating a patient. If I had been in your place, emotionally involved, I'm sure I'd have been sucked in too."

"Come off it! You're talking to me the way you did when I was your patient and you were trying to build up my confidence. Please, Dick, don't do that."

"Believe me, I'm not. I'm being totally serious. It's clear

from everything you've told me about this fellow McCormick that he falls into a well-known psychological classification. He's an example par excellence of the psychopath."

Michael stopped in front of the Harvard boathouse. "That's a person without a conscience. How can that help me?"

"Well," Landey sighed, wiping the sweat from his forehead, "What you've said is true. But that's only the theoretical definition. When you translate that into reality, you come up with an individual similar to McCormick who manipulates others' behavior."

Anderson raised his eyebrows and replied skeptically, "You'll have to be more specific."

"A psychopath sounds totally convincing, but he's exactly like a chameleon, except that instead of changing colors a psychopath changes values and attitudes at will. All depending on his goals at the time. I'm sure McCormick comes across as genuinely sincere regardless of who he's talking to."

"You're right about that."

"It's mind-blowing when you see someone who's a master at it. To one group of people, he'll be running off at the mouth expressing one opinion, to another he'll be equally as relaxed and confident, spewing forth a completely opposite point of view on the very same topic. If you're sitting in the room with a psychopath as skilled as McCormick sounds, you'd begin questioning your own perceptions, your own sense of reality." Landey paused briefly. "Never questioning his."

Landey began jogging again, this time more rapidly. Anderson surprised himself by the ease with which he kept pace.

The psychiatrist went on. "The danger by now should be obvious. An unexpected development occurs. McCormick, not experiencing guilt, remorse, or self-doubt, smoothly shifts tactics. Therefore, he's always one step ahead of everybody else. He directs all his energies towards his all-consuming goal. The means needed to arrive at the desired end are irrelevant and constantly in a state of flux. With his charm and intelligence, before you know it, a psychopath has you by the balls. Everyone viewed as the enemy, yet all view him as their ally. Believe me, they're a malignant species."

Anderson's eyes lit up. "You've described McCormick perfectly. Your personality profile on him will help tremendously. By understanding how he operates, we'll be able to render him ineffective."

"Not so fast," Landey said. "It's not going to be that easy. Who's we?"

"Russell! He'll listen."

"Mike, for you to believe that, means you haven't really digested what I've said."

"I don't follow."

"Russell believes you're dead. By now, McCormick has the president sucked into his master plan and eating out of his hands."

"You underestimate the president."

Landey shook his head. "No, you underestimate McCormick."

Anderson, dismayed asked, "Well, then, if you were in my place, what would you do?"

"Forget about getting help."

Anderson suddenly stopped running. "Why?"

"You're aware of how McCormick's mind works, his methods, the techniques he uses. No one else is. That's the problem. Nobody will believe you. I mean nobody."

"I can't go it alone."

"You must. You don't have a choice. You're meeting with Wilkinson tomorrow evening. I'm sure he's been taken in by McCormick. He'll try to convince you there's nothing significant in the doctor's dossier. Don't be put off. Press him to tell you what's in his file. There'll be certain facts in his background that should alert you. Trust your perceptions. Follow them up. You have one big advantage over McCormick. Psychopaths can lie, deceive, and manipulate, but facts don't lie. Psychopaths can't change them."

"You sound very confident. I hope you're right," Anderson said as they started jogging again.

Twenty-two

Every evening from an office in the ocher-colored neo-Renaissance headquarters at 2 Dzerzhinsky Square, a mile from the Kremlin, Konstantine I. Sverdlov, the head of the KGB, peered out the window and stared at the statue of Felix Dzerzhinsky, the first head of the Soviet Secret Police, standing guard in the courtyard below.

This evening the full-faced general smiled contentedly as he contemplated how smoothly everything had been going in his organization's top assignment.

Sverdlov's spirits had soared since he received word the New York doctor had been eliminated. With that obstacle out of the way, he was confident his present task would be successfully completed. Once accomplished his political future had no bounds.

With 700,000 agents and an equal number of informers, compared to the United States intelligence and counterintelligence network of only 130,000, Cold War successors had often been the rule rather than the exception.

Until now, Sverdlov's greatest personal accomplishment had to do with Line espionage. Over the years, he had slowly and methodically planted 20,000 Soviet and East Block agents throughout the United States: in the high-tech corridor stretching from Boston to Baltimore, in southern California's aerospace industries, and in San Francisco's Silicon Valley.

His promotion to head the KGB came as the result of his agents stealing two projection mask aligners made by the Perkin-Elmer Corporation of Norwalk, Connecticut. The aligners are automobile-size machines called Micragign 200s that are used in the manufacture of microcircuitry for everything from digital watches to missile guidance systems.

Although success had catapulted him into his present position, the importance of that project paled in comparison to the enormity of the project he was now spearheading.

However, should a snag occur and the mission fail, he realized his fate would not be the usual one. It would be far worse than being shipped off to Siberia.

"This matter should never have gotten to this point," Cullie Hamilton said, striking the palm of his hand on the walnut conference table. "Imagine the president of these United States dictating his plan to us. What in God's name happened to our democratic ways?"

Kingsley, anxiously adjusting his wire frames, replied, "Cullie, we've rehashed this over and over again. You know damn well how this came about. The choice was simple: another meaningless meeting between our two countries or the chance finally to accomplish something significant with regard to world peace. We opted for the latter. To ensure this result, we agreed with Russell: He and Molonyn were to iron out all details, meet secretly, and report back to their respective countries once they reached an agreement that would be acceptable to both countries. Don't forget, we didn't plan on Russell's health becoming the crucial issue."

Gabe Condon, the Speaker of the House, interjected, provoked beyond endurance. "Cullie, will you knock it off?"

Blandly ignoring him, Cullie Hamilton repeated, "Mr.

Speaker, sir, as I've said, I never would have agreed to a summit meeting under these circumstances. It's too damn risky. Why in God's name do we have to support the president in all his wild adventures, no matter what? Even if his health were fine, I'd have voted against this plan, and I think a lot of others here would have joined me. That's all I can say. When we were consulted, the facts weren't all on the table. I know Russell's a great public servant, but I don't think it's good to entrust so much power to any one human being."

Kingsley replied impatiently, "Cullie, stop exaggerating! You're accomplishing nothing but getting everyone riled up. The bottom line is that we do have control. That's why this committee was formed. Believe me, Russell won't go to the summit if we decide he's not fit to go. Now"—Kingsley turned and stared at the majority leader's protruding eyes— "with your permission, may we proceed? I met with the president yesterday. The location for the summit has been set. Russell and Molonyn will be meeting in Lucerne, Switzerland. The specific dates have yet to be worked out."

"Why Lucerne?" the attorney general asked.

"It's a long story," Kingsley began. "It's Russell's idea. Supposedly in 1291 along the banks of Lake Lucerne there was a legendary meeting that led to the founding of the Confederacy in Switzerland which has endured and resulted in peace for more than seven hundred years. Their meeting will take place in the meadow of Rutli on the west bank of Lake Lucerne. In August 1291, the different provinces of Switzerland —Schwyz, Uri, Nadwalder, and Untorwalden—met and formed an alliance on that identical spot. They worked out a way to settle all disagreements among themselves by arbitration. They promised to resort to these laws rather than to violence. This was confirmed by oath and sealed by a document which inaugurated the Swiss Confederacy that we know today. The president felt that this spot, which symbolizes everlasting nonviolent ways of settling disagreements, would be the ideal location for the summit, for the two world leaders to work out a US-USSR nuclear disarmament pact and a method for dealing with future contingencies peacefully rather than through war."

"I know you don't want my opinion, so with all due respect to the vice-president, I'll bow out on this matter. That leaves Russell's health as my main concern. I won't make waves in this committee if you convince me Russell can successfully pull this off," Cullie replied, his hands folded across his massive chest.

Kingsley eyed McCormick. "Doctor, you heard Senator Hamilton. What's your medical opinion?"

McCormick, seated erect in his chair replied, "I can readily understand the senator's concern. The president shouldn't be allowed to meet with Molonyn unless he's physically and mentally up to it. As I've said before, there is no doubt that Russell is suffering from Alzheimer's disease, a progressive form of senility. I've been examing him daily, studying his behavior and checking his stamina. At this point, we are fortunate in that the president, while showing minor changes, has yet to reach the point where his symptoms are apparent. Gentlemen, don't forget my reputation is on the line as well as yours. If Russell's symptoms pointed towards a significant degree of deterioration and I neglected to pick them up, I'd be unfit to be his personal physician." McCormick waited for his words to have the impact he desired. He glanced around the conference table, studying the eight members of the committee. When he felt certain his message had registered, he continued. "Russell talks to me freely. It's apparent the Russians trust him and that they are as ignorant of his difficulties as the American people are. I know I may be out of line, but I believe it will take years, perhaps generations, before we're able to build up the goodwill that Russell and Molonyn have already established. Gentlemen, the president can make it. I'll be with him in Lucerne twenty-four hours a day monitoring his health. If at any time I feel he's less alert, becoming fatigued, or in any way losing his grasp of the situation, I'll call and notify the committee. Then, based on your recommendations, I'll convince the president to postpone or cancel the meeting."

Kingsley looked around the room. "Any comments?"

"As I have said before, Kingsley, that doctor is one smart cookie." Cullie Hamilton turned and faced McCormick. "What you're sayin' is that the sooner the summit is held the better. Tell me, son, that is your point, isn't it?"

McCormick nodded in agreement.

"Then what are we all waitin' for? There doesn't seem to be much of a choice. McCormick has given a good argument for us to press Russell into making the date as soon as possible. Monday is Labor Day. Anyone have a preference?"

Kingsley broke in. "The Labor Day weekend strikes me as the ideal time for such a meeting to take place. After that, the summer will be over, everyone will be getting back into their regular routine and that includes scrutinizing the news. Right now, most of the country's top reporters are on vacation, their minds on other matters, while the American people are busy preparing for their weekend barbecues and bidding farewell to the summer. This weekend everybody's attention will be focused elsewhere, away from Washington and away from world events. Russell needs three days for the summit. He'd have to be back at the White House by Tuesday."

"That doesn't give us much time," answered the Speaker of the House, his eyes glowing in the incandescent reflections of light. "Today's Wednesday. That leaves only two days until the weekend."

"I know all that," said Kingsley, refusing to cower under Gabe Condon's stare. "Russell must be in Lucerne by Friday morning. That gives him two days to get ready."

"That's a lot to pull off in less than forty-eight hours," said Hamilton, puffing on a Sir Walter Raleigh. "But it's worth a try. I'm game. Count me in."

The rest of the committee members nodded in agreement.

"How are you going to convince Russell to go along with our decision?" questioned the attorney general.

Kingsley, his lined face haggard, his voice strained, replied, "That's not going to be the problem. The hurdle will be the Soviet premier. Russell is going to have to convince Molonyn that their meeting should be held this weekend, and he must present it in such a way as not to arouse the premier's suspicions." The vice-president reached across the table for a glass of ice water, took several sips, and continued, "Cullie, I think we'd better go and pay Russell a visit. We've got a lot to discuss."

Kingsley got up from his chair and stood in front of the rest of the committee. "Well, gentlemen, keep your fingers crossed. We'll reconvene next week and either congratulate ourselves or begin to pick up the pieces." Looking at McCormick, he continued, "Everything hinges on our having judged Russell's physical condition accurately."

"Your punctuality doesn't make up for your bad taste," Wilkinson snapped, looking up from the table and glancing around the unattractive dining room.

Anderson sipped his martini and edged forward in his seat. "What did you find out?"

"Just as I figured, nothing."

"Please tell me what was in his file. Let me judge its significance."

Wilkinson shrugged his broad shoulders. "McCormick, an only child, was born in Russia. His family came to the States shortly after the Second World War. Art was eleven. His father wanted a new beginning, a fresh start. You know, America is still called the land of opportunity."

Anderson interrupted, "What! McCormick is Russian?"

Wilkinson's annoyance surfaced. "What's the big deal? There are thousands of Americans whose ancestors came from the Soviet Union. Don't forget we were all once immigrants. I'm only a third-generation American myself. My family originally came from Lithuania. Our name was anglicized so that we'd have an easier time being assimilated into the mainstream of the country."

"Okay. I get your point. Please continue."

"McCormick's family settled in Flossmoor, Illinois, a suburb near Chicago. His father never quite made a success out of the real-estate business and couldn't afford to send him to medical school. That's where the armed forces entered the picture. The army was willing to finance his medical education. Art in return had to pay them back by spending several years working as a medical officer in the army. He apparently grew to like the work as well as the life-style and decided to make it a career. He's been stationed at various bases both in this country and abroad. For the past several years he has been at Walter Reed." Wilkinson paused. "That's all there is. I told you, you're barking up the wrong tree."

Suddenly everything made sense, the parts fitting together to form a whole, a picture more frightening than Anderson had imagined. "I don't think so," Anderson replied angrily. "I won't accept that." He glared at Wilkinson. "Don't you see you've supplied me with the link that's been missing? Let me explain what's been going on. Russell was ill. He called me in. I examined him and took some X-rays. Then I was attacked in my office by Brian Steele, a hit man I believe was hired by McCormick. I could never figure out why. Now I know. McCormick wanted Russell's skull X-ray. That X-ray was the one concrete piece of evidence that pointed to the president having a different illness than the one McCormick wanted tagged on him. Ragland then began badgering McCormick about his indifferent attitude towards the president's deteriorating health. Knowing Brent, he probably threatened to have him replaced as Russell's doctor unless he shaped up. McCormick couldn't tolerate that development, so he had Steele kill Ragland. I was the next intended victim because I was trying to figure out what was wrong with the president. McCormick obviously realized it would only be a matter of time until I hit on the truth. Fortunately I survived the accident that was meant to kill me. McCormick believed I was dead and thought he was safe. Therefore, he had to get rid of the only person who could connect him to these events. Hence he killed Steele.

"However, as they say, God works in mysterious ways. After my accident I would up in Clarkson Hospital in Virginia, the same hospital the president supposedly had been evaluated in. I got into the hospital record room looking for Russell's chart, and lo and behold, what did I find? A different chart. McCormick had pulled a clever one. He had taken the record of a patient who indeed had Alzheimer's disease, removed its contents, and placed it in Russell's file. Presto chango, there it is for all to see. Russell had been worked up and did have Alzheimer's after all.

"Armed with this evidence I contacted the reporter Eric Dawson. Dawson then confronted McCormick. I discovered Dawson's dead body in his home. McCormick, believing I've been killed in the car accident, is at this very moment savoring victory."

Wilkinson interrupted. "Enough already! You're crazy!"

"I'm not finished. While all these events are happening, the real purpose for McCormick's actions remain elusive. That is, until your report. McCormick, as you yourself have stated, is a Russian."

Wilkinson again interrupted. "He was born in Russia. He's an American citizen. A model one at that."

Anderson, ignoring Wilkinson's remark, continued, "McCormick is involved in getting Russell to a secret meeting that Russell himself and Premier Molonyn of the Soviet Union have arranged. He's making sure the president will be in a weakened and vulnerable state physically and mentally during the stressful negotiations. As the hours tick by, according to McCormick's plan, Molonyn would gradually wear Russell down. Eventually the president would submit to the premier's persuasive arguments, with the resultant effect on the United States disastrous. In effect, Russell would have inadvertently sold our country down the tubes."

"I repeat, you're mad! Mad as a hatter. I've never even heard about any secret meetings and surely the State Department would know if there was anything wrong with the president's health."

"Damn it, Wilkinson! Listen to me! McCormick has orchestrated a great cold war ploy."

The undersecretary leaned forward. "You've seen too many spy films. Now that you've had your say, kindly knock it off." He motioned to the waiter. "Let's eat."

Anderson, stunned, sat silently. He couldn't believe his ears. He had presented Wilkinson with evidence to substantiate what might become the most significant covert event since World War II, and the second ranking officer in the State Department had completely tossed it aside, labeling it absurd.

Suddenly Anderson remembered his conversation with Dick Landey. "McCormick is a superb psychopath. No one will believe you. Go with your perceptions. Trust them."

McCormick, Russian born and bred, was aiding the Russian cause. Anderson had to stop him before it was too late. And he had to do it alone.

Twenty-three

NEVER IN HIS LIFE DID HE RECALL FEELING THIS HAPPY, this satisfied. Not as a child growing up in Moscow and certainly not since he was eleven when his father convinced the youngster to let the Golandropovs adopt him and move with them to America to a small town on the outskirts of Chicago. How he had hated those first few years in America. The outsider, never included, words heard, not understood. It had taken agonizing work, but the long hard hours spent with his tutor had finally paid off. By the time he was seventeen and a freshman at the University of Michigan nobody knew he was a foreigner. He spoke English fluently, all traces of an accent gone. He became a leader, a student others looked up to and admired. But he never felt he truly belonged. His heart remained in Russia. In the years that followed he perfected his skills, became a respected doctor, but he still longed to return to his native land, to his home, to his real parents.

How proud his father would be when he'd find out his son had successfully accomplished what had been asked of him. He had been given the supreme opportunity to serve the ultimate cause and had handled it masterfully. The years of painstaking effort had been worth it. He'd finally gain his father's long sought-after approval.

Art McCormick, born Alexei Andreev, seated in his green Audi 5000 was slowly winding his way through the renovated section of Alexandria, reminiscing and smiling. He had to admit he'd done one hell of a good job. Once this mission was completed, he was certain a hero's welcome would await him back in Russia. The turbo-charged car passed Cameron Mews, the colonial townhouse development that exemplified Alexandria's approach to new housing in Old Town. Two blocks later at the intersection of Washington Street and Cameron lay his destination—the home of much of the Russian delegation, and of Yuri Karpov, the Russian ambassador to the United States.

"The ambassador is expecting you. Please follow me," the butler announced, leading McCormick into the dimly lit oak-paneled den.

"Comrade Andreev, glad you could make it on such short notice," the tall, beefy ambassador said, pressing down the tufts of white hair that circled his otherwise bald head with his left hand while shaking McCormick's outstretched arm with his right. "Care to join me? I've been feasting on blini and some delicious caviar."

"No thanks. I'll pass."

"Good for you. That's why you stay as trim as you do. Come sit down." Karpov motioned to a nearby sofa. "We became alarmed when that Dr. Anderson began poking around."

"You're not the only one. That's why I had to have him eliminated."

Karpov nodded his head. "Well done, Alexei, well done." He bent over, scooped up a healthy portion of caviar with his finger and in one mouthful devoured the delicacy. "What's Russell's current medical status?"

"He's going downhill. I've been examining him daily. Each

time I pick up subtle but definite signs of increased deterioration: his attention span lower, his ability to concentrate lessened, his memory faltering. I don't think anything will deter us from obtaining a nuclear disarmament treaty greatly in our favor. Our future position in the world will be stronger than the one we obtained at Yalta."

"Ah, excellent. Peace sealed and delivered for the entire world to see, but with terms that will result in a strong, powerful Union of Soviet Socialist Republics and a weak, impotent United States. Everything will be firmly in place waiting for the proper time. When we're through, the Western world will be ours. The feats of the old Roman Empire will pale in comparison."

The ambassador draped his right arm over the upholstered sofa. "Alexei, we are so close to our goal. But," he paused, "everything will be for nothing if the president backs down. That's why I summoned you so urgently. The premier is fearful. He knows Russell's no fool. He's weak, and he knows it. Molonyn is afraid that if we wait too much longer Russell will realize he's not up to attending the summit. We can't take that risk. The premier wants the summit moved up. Play on Russell's fears. You've got to convince him that the sooner the meetings are held, the greater his chances of being fully alert and on top of things will be. Impress on him that with each passing day his capabilities are diminishing."

"Ambassador, I believe we're in luck. You know that committee on Capitol Hill that I told you about?"

"Yes. What of it?"

"They met earlier today. I convinced them that Russell's currently able to handle himself well, but if the summit isn't held shortly the chances that the president will be able to function satisfactorily will be greatly reduced."

"And their reaction to your proposal?"

"They latched on to it. Vice-President Kingsley and Senator

Hamilton are to meet with the president. They're going to be doing our work for us. They want the president to be at the Lucerne meeting with the premier this weekend."

Ambassador Karpov's eyes lit up. "The premier will be delighted."

"Tell Premier Molonyn not to worry. Russell has complete faith in me. I'll be with the president on Air Force One. We'll leave for Lucerne no later than tomorrow night."

"Good work, Alexei, good work."

The two men eyed the president. Kingsley spoke first. "Mr. President, our committee met today."

"Yes, Bart? Go ahead."

"There are certain details we feel we must know."

"I said I'd cooperate. What are they?"

"Have you spoken to Mr. Molonyn recently?" Hamilton wailed.

"Yes. Today in fact."

"Have the dates been set for your meeting?" the vice-president inquired.

"Not the specific date, but it probably will be sometime in October. The premier and I have worked it out so we're both prepared if need be to leave for Lucerne on a day's notice."

"So, Mr. President, sir, if I heard you correctly, you could meet with Mr. Molonyn in a few days."

"Tomorrow, if necessary," Russell answered. "Why?"

"I don't know if we've mentioned that McCormick has been sitting in on our meetings," Kingsley said.

"You have."

"He supports your decision to attend the summit, but at the same time, he is concerned about your health."

Russell broke in. "I know. He's a good man." The president momentarily thought about Anderson. "I've learned to rely on McCormick's judgment."

"That's good, because Art believes the sooner you hold the summit, the better it will be," Kingsley replied.

"If that's McCormick's stance, it's fine with me. That won't present any problems. I'm all prepared. The agenda's set."

"Then you're willing to move up the date?"

"Yes."

"Then perhaps you'll consider holding the meeting this holiday weekend. Nobody will realize you're out of the country. We'll cover for you."

"That's short notice, but it can be arranged."

Kingsley sighed in relief.

"What else?" Russell asked, eyebrows raised.

Cullie lit up a cigar, took two puffs and coughed before speaking. "You mentioned the agenda. We'd all feel more secure knowin' in advance what you're plannin' on discussin'."

"Only if you give your word that what I say stays in this room."

The two men nodded in agreement.

"Molonyn and I are prepared to lay all our cards on the table. We mean *all*. Otherwise the meeting will be worthless. We're going to discuss everything involved with nuclear aggression."

Kingsley and Hamilton glanced at one another, taken by surprise at the extent both sides appeared willing to go. "That's quite an undertakin'," Hamilton said.

"Molonyn and I are aware of that."

"You're to be commended on the enormity of your efforts, Mr. President, sir. We've got one more matter here to discuss, and then we'll leave you in peace."

"What's that?" Russell queried.

"While you're in Lucerne, we want McCormick to be with you at all times. Trust him. Open up to him. Confide in him fully. He's the only one who understands both your medical condition and what you're tryin' to accomplish. If at any time you feel you're gettin' run down, or in any way slippin', tell McCormick. He has orders to contact us. As I'm sure you can understand, Mr. President, we can't afford—"

Russell interrupted, his voice firm. "You can tell your committee they have nothing to worry about. I'll keep McCormick completely informed at all times during the meeting. I may have a big ego, but my primary loyalty is to my country's welfare."

The three men stood for a moment in the Oval Office, looking at one another. Finally Russell walked to his desk and picked up the bright red telephone lying next to the black one. "Now, gentlemen. If you'll excuse me, I've got to get Premier Molonyn on the line."

Part Three

Twenty-four

THE JET LINER PIERCED THE THICK BLANKET OF LOW lying clouds, the snow-capped tops of Mount Rigi and Mount Pilatus now visible.

President Russell, seated near the front of Air Force One, gazed out the window as the large vessel continued its smooth descent. The underside of the clouds was flat and featureless, like a sheet of mirror reflecting the wet concrete of the runway below. The town of Lucerne in the distance, its shape fitting snugly into the curve of its lake, the city of little streets, secret gardens, boulevards, and the magnificent chapel bridge with its imposing thirteenth-century octagonal water tower. As the presidential plane continued its descent, Russell could see the roads behind the city winding their way up into the lush green hills and forests, climbing ever higher into the mountains beyond. Farther in the distance, too far to be seen, lay Russell's destination, the meadows of Rutli.

With a sudden lurch forward, the airplane touched down. A quarter of a mile along the apron, another jet surrounded by service vehicles was parked. It was an Ilyushin jet, Premier Molonyn's plane. The president had wanted to arrive first. To present an aura of being settled, in control. Obviously, his desire hadn't materialized. Russell could only hope that wouldn't be a harbinger of things to come.

For the first time, the president questioned the wisdom of holding the summit at such a remote place, a long, tortuous ride over narrow mountainous roads. A grueling task, if conditions were ideal, but in his present weary state. . . . His cottage in Seelesberg, Molonyn's in Treib, the meadow of Rutli a stone's throw between the two villages. Nothing could be more symbolic than this picturesque historical site. Yet . . . wasn't Switzerland herself sufficiently symbolic? Her name was synonomous with neutrality and peace. Lucerne, acessible and serene, would have provided the significance both men were striving for.

Russell shrugged his shoulders. The president knew he was the one who pressed for Rutli, not Molonyn. The premier had preferred a more convenient spot, one with more creature comforts. It was Russell who had stressed symbolic meaning and downplayed Molonyn's reservations. Therefore, Rutli it would be.

McCormick leaned across the aisle and faced the president. "We'll be disembarking in about ten minutes, Mr. President."

Russell rubbed his eyes, his fatigue apparent. "McCormick, I don't have to tell you that what I'm embarking on is the single most important event of my life."

"Yes, Mr. President, I'm well aware of that."

"But since Anderson's death, I don't have much stamina and I'm more forgetful. Without him, I somehow feel lost. He was always there when I needed him. Always . . . until now. I don't know . . . the stress of the summit. Maybe Kingsley and the rest of them were right all along. Maybe it is too much for me."

"I know how you feel, but I'm your doctor, and I know what you can and cannot do. Believe me, you're completely capable of handling yourself at the meetings. Now please stop worrying. We've got a long ride ahead of us."

McCormick opened a bottle of Corton-Charlemagre, grabbed two glasses, filled them and handed one to the president. "Mr. President, with your permission I'd like to make a toast. To success at the summit, for you, sir, and for the United States."

A look of relief spread across McCormick's face as their glasses met, a look that went unnoticed.

Landey's advice had led nowhere. Anderson had spent the major portion of the day blocked in his attempt to stop McCormick by the need "to go it alone." All he had succeeded in doing was heightening his already significant degree of helplessness. He knew what he desperately wanted to do: reach Russell and lay everything out on the table. Landey and the rest of them be damned. But each time he geared himself to act, he vacillated, fearful of what he'd do if Russell reacted as Wilkinson did, as Landey convincingly argued everyone would do. Anderson would have played out his hand and lost. He couldn't afford to do that. He needed a trump card before taking the plunge.

Anderson flipped the X-ray screen back on and stared once again at Russell's skull series, those pictures that showed beyond doubt a shift of the pineal gland, the evidence he needed to support his claim that McCormick was linked with a massive cover-up, that a conspiracy was presently in progress.

The more Michael looked at the X-rays, the more hopeless he felt. The mass in his friend's brain was evolving, its growth rate unpredictable, its nature still unknown. What good was this visual documentation? What good was his vast store of medical knowledge when all attempts at helping Russell were blocked by forces beyond his control?

Frank Stanton had read the X-rays, had warned Anderson

of the seriousness of the problem, the need for rapid evaluation and treatment. That was more than two weeks ago. Weeks where everything should have been completed, weeks when nothing was done.

Anderson suddenly switched his attention from the X-rays to Stanton. What would the radiologist do if placed in similar circumstances? Stanton was known as the ultimate pragmatist, often breaching protocol if he deemed it medically indicated. His refusal to play hospital politics had cost him dearly. He'd been kept off the powerful hospital governing board. Yet his willingness to charge forward irrespective of consequences had saved many a patient's life.

Perhaps he should call Stanton. Anderson had turned to him once, why not again?

He threaded his way past the examining table and picked up the telephone suspended on the wall.

"Hello, Stanton? It's Anderson."

"Mike, where the hell have you been? I called your service the other day. They told me you're still signed out. What gives?"

"I need your help," Anderson replied, his tone urgent. "Remember those X-rays I asked you to read?"

"Sure. How could I have forgotten? I'd never seen you looking so harried, so worried. What did the mass turn out to be?"

"That's why I'm calling. I still don't have the answer."

"What! You must be kidding!"

"No, I'm serious."

Stanton, startled, said, "Somebody is walking around with a time bomb ticking away just waiting to explode and you're telling me nothing's been done? Mike, that's not like you. You're usually on top of things. What's happened?"

Anderson inhaled deeply. "It's a very delicate matter. Not your usual case."

"What the hell difference does that make?"

"I didn't tell you at the time, but the films are President Russell's."

There was a momentary silence at the other end of the line. Finally Stanton spoke. "You're telling me President Russell is living with that mass in his brain and you've done absolutely nothing about it?"

"I've tried to do a lot, but my hands are tied."

"How so?" Stanton inquired.

"It's a very involved, messy situation. All tangled up in psychological factors and poltitical ramifications. Basically, though, what it boils down to is that Russell's not officially my patient."

"Then how'd you get involved in the first place?"

"We're old friends. He called me in to help."

"I don't understand what's so damn complicated, then. You just said it yourself. He asked for your help. I take it you believe his treating physician is missing the boat."

"It's far worse than that. I have reasons to believe—"

Stanton interrupted. "Mike, I don't want to hear all the nuances. I've learned that too many intricate details can screw up the most logical mind. Listening to various experts, each with their well-thought-out approach. You know what happens? You begin weighing one factor against another, comparing the relative importance of the various variables involved. The result: mental paralysis. You're a doctor, a damned good one. You know what's best for Russell, no one else does. If I were you, I'd say damn all those ivory-tower types. You know what happened while Nero fiddled."

Anderson sighed in relief. "Thanks, Frank. I think that's just what I needed to hear."

Russell sank back on the bed, pulled the blanket over his shoulders, and settled his head into the down pillow. "Some house, huh," he said, turning to face McCormick. "Here it is, still summer and the place feels more like late fall." The president glanced around the bedroom, with its low beam ceiling and the tightly drawn curtains that only served to make the room damp, not warmer. In front of him was a large wardrobe, the doors entirely covered by tinted glass. "I'm bushed. I never thought we'd make it. Those roads. The distance from Lucerne. It's all so medieval, not at all twentieth-century."

"That's very true, Mr. President, but the setting is exactly what you wanted," McCormick replied.

"Sometimes I wonder about myself. Those last twelve miles fron Stans to Seelesberg must have taken an hour."

McCormick chuckled. "I must admit, Mr. President, to having butterflies during that stretch. I don't think I've ever traveled on a steeper or more winding road in my life."

"Neither have I."

McCormick couldn't allow Russell's confidence to ebb, at least not yet. "But, I must commend you, sir. The picturesque setting, its virgin beauty; it would take a poet to do it justice. This is the most exquisite spot I've ever been to. I believe the trip was well worth it."

"Art, how far are we from Lucerne?"

"I'm not sure, but forty miles seems about right."

Russell replied, shaking his head. "That's quite something. Forty miles in three hours. I used to be able to bicycle faster than that."

McCormick smiled. "I think that's why most people leave their cars in Lucerne and either take one of the steamers that run on the lake or use the combined rail and cableway system through the mountains. Don't forget, we're at an altitude of twenty-five hundred feet."

"Could that be contributing to my exhaustion?"

"Quite possibly, but your system will adjust. Don't forget, Molonyn will be operating under similar circumstances."

"But he's not sick. At least, not that I know of."

Russell lifted himself off the bed and onto an easy chair. "Did you know that every year on the first of August, Switzerland celebrates its independence day? On that day, Swiss citizens gather in the meadow where Molonyn and I will be meeting and reaffirm their allegiance to the principle of the alliance, an alliance that's lasted seven hundred years. That is what all this bother and secrecy is all about. The premier and I have set our sights on rivaling what the Swiss confederacy accomplished in 1291. But," Russell's voice trailed off, "that's a tall order, and I'm already knocked out."

McCormick walked over to the president. "You have three hours before you and the premier are scheduled to start your talks. I know you want to go over some of your briefs. How about devoting an hour to them, followed by a shower and a nap? After that, You'll be refreshed and ready to go."

Russell looked McCormick in the eye. "I hope you're right. I only hope you're right."

"Mr. President, follow my instructions to the letter, and I'm convinced you'll handle yourself perfectly. First, you must get proper rest. Second, I ordered you a special diet consisting of additional supplements of vitamins and minerals; third, I'm going to give you a daily injection of choline, a medication proven effective in enhancing memory; and fourth and most important, if it's at all possible, I'd like to be named unofficial chief of staff during these meetings. This way I'll be in a position to screen all calls, messages, and visitors, as well as direct the Secret Service. I'd like to be able to do everything to ease your burden so you're free to concentrate solely on the negotiations." McCormick paused. "Of course, Mr. President, it's just a suggestion. It's up to you whether to grant me these powers or not."

Russell nodded his head in agreement. "It's a good idea. Just promise me that I'll have the necessary physical and mental strength to deal with Molonyn."

"Mr. President, it's a promise."

Twenty-five

It had been a sleepless night. Anderson tossing and turning, waiting for morning, a man alone racing in a maze for survival. Survival for Russell. He looked through his bedroom window; across the street pale sunshine washed the cream-colored stones of the city's old buildings. The clock on his night table registered eight-thirteen. It was time to spring into action.

Stanton had supplied the encouragement Anderson had needed, the extra shove to thrust him forward. He would call the president, explain everything, the misdiagnosis, Ragland's murder, the investigative reporter's death, even his own presumed fatal car crash. He'd lay it out for the president to assimilate. After Russell fully digested those facts, Anderson would disclose the worst: that his own personal physician, Dr. Art McCormick, born Alexei Andreev, was the executioner, the mastermind behind these terrible events. His purpose, to shift the balance of power toward the Soviet Union. He envisioned Russell rejoicing at knowing his best friend was alive, his euphoria overshadowing any brainwashing McCormick had been able to do.

But if, after hearing Anderson's warning, Russell persisted in going along with McCormick, so be it. This time, events would turn out differently. Regardless of barriers thrown up or opposition encountered, nothing was going to prevent Anderson from tearing Russell away from McCormick's malignant grip and to see to it that the president received the medical help he so desperately needed.

Anderson got up from his bed and stretched, rotating his neck, the muscle tension receding. It was now eight-thirty. Russell would be busy at work in the Oval Office. Quickly he dialed the president's private line, using the letters HEARSES, the word that in happier, more carefree times had stood for the two vehicles he and John used in order to drive their fraternity brothers to and from the Yale Bowl during the football season. Now, the same word carried a different, far more ominous meaning.

The phone rang several times. Anderson waited, his concern deepening as each ring went unanswered. After four rings, Russell was to pick up, that had been their signal for years. There had been occasions when Russell was in conference and couldn't be disturbed. At those times, if a call was important enough and Anderson could contain his impatience, he'd stay on the line and eventually the call would be rerouted to another private line, this one in the president's bedroom. Somebody, usually Peg's secretary, would answer and relay the message to Russell. This time, circumstances were different. Did he dare risk speaking to anybody but Russell? Everyone believed Anderson was dead. The shock of finding out Anderson was alive shouldn't come from a third party. The impact of hearing the news could conceivably jolt the president more than his precarious state could withstand.

He was about to hang up and try later when he remembered Stanton's advice. The radiologist was right. Time was too crucial to consider psychological bullshit.

Finally, after the eleventh ring, the phone was picked up.

"Thank God somebody answered. I thought the White House was deserted."

"Who's this?" a groggy female voice yawned into the receiver.

"It's Mike Anderson."

Peg Russell awoke with a start. "Is this some sort of practical joke?"

"No. It's really me."

"But you were killed in a car crash!"

"I was meant to be killed in that crash, but I survived. I don't have time to explain now. I must talk to John."

"I'm sorry, but that's impossible. He's not here."

"When will he be back?"

"Not for a few days."

"Where is he?"

"I can't say."

Anderson pleaded. "Peg, you must! John's life is at stake. You might not love him, but I know you don't want to be responsible for killing him."

"What are you talking about?"

"I'll tell you later. I only want to save your husband's life and to do that I need your help. You've got to trust me."

"I'm so confused. First you're dead. Now, you're not only alive, but scaring me."

Anderson's voice bristled. "It's time you woke up! If it takes frightening you to do that, those are the breaks. Now, where is your husband?"

"In Lucerne."

"Oh, my God," Anderson's voice dropped, his stomach sank. A turn of events he hadn't anticipated, that he wasn't prepared for. He paused to regain his composure. "Did McCormick press you to convince the president that he couldn't afford to wait any longer before holding the summit, that to be capable of functioning well he'd better move the negotiations up, even if it meant leaving immediately?" Anderson drew a deep breath before continuing. "Peg, I know how you feel about McCormick. But, you must put your feelings aside, for your husband's sake and for the good of the country. I need your answer."

Peg, stunned, replied, "Yes. Art did insist on my talking to John, but you've got things twisted around. He did it for John's sake and for the country's welfare."

"Peg, you're a stubborn woman. Words won't convince you that I'm right. That your lover, I'm sorry, your male friend is plotting against Russell and against the United States. You're going to have to see that for yourself. Where in Lucerne are the meetings to be held?"

"Outside Lucerne, in the meadows of Rutli."

"I've been to Lucerne often, but never to Rutli."

"It's a two- to three-hour drive from Lucerne."

"I don't believe it. Is your husband staying there?"

"No. He and McCormick are staying in Seelesberg, a small village less than a mile from Rutli."

"Oh, that's just great! Rutli is remote enough, but at least I think it's on Lake Lucerne. Seelesberg is a half a mile straight up the mountain. They couldn't have settled on a more inaccessible spot if they'd tried." Anderson, wearied, sat down on his bed, "We've got to hope that your husband can last until we get there."

"You're crazy! His life isn't in danger! McCormick is with him, taking care of him."

"I'm not going to waste precious time trying to convince you that John's life is in danger. You owe me a favor. This is the time I want it repaid."

"What do you want me to do?"

"I need a private jet to take us to Lucerne and a car to meet us on our arrival, preferably a small one with front-wheel drive. Navigating those roads can be maddening."

"How can I possibly get my hands on a jet? John has taken the only plane I have at my disposal."

"You must know someone with enough clout to get what we need. Contact him. Tell him you have to have a jet at the National Airport in Alexandria, say, by four P.M. That gives you seven hours to make the necessary arrangements. Can you get away without alerting the Secret Service?"

"Of course not!"

"How many men will the agency insist on?"

"Probably two."

"Can you choose which two?"

"Yes."

"Then choose two you know and trust. I'll meet you at the airport. Your husband's health is being used as a pawn by the Russians. We've got to get to Lucerne, to Seelesberg, before either Russell or the United States suffers permanent and irreversible damage."

"You're being melodramatic. But I do owe you, so I'll see you at National at four P.M."

McCormick crossed the path at the rear of the cottage, making sure he wasn't noticed by the Secret Servicemen, who were fortunately preoccupied with mapping out their protective plans for the president while he was in Seelesberg. He climbed a steep incline and entered a small tavern. The tables were empty except for a bald, heavyset man seated near the rear of the room digging into a cheese omelet and gulping down a glass of white wine.

"I know I'm not to ask your name, but do come over. From what I gather, I'm sure you could use a drink."

"Thanks just the same, but I still have work to do." Mc-

Cormick reached into his trouser pocket and pulled out an envelope. "It's all in there. Count it if you wish."

The portly man pointed to an archaic wall phone at the opposite end of the room. "That's what you paid for."

McCormick picked up the receiver and began dialing. "The president's taking a nap. He's put me in complete command. Nobody, nothing can gain access to him without first going through me. The rest, Premier Molonyn, depends on you."

Kate Robins was combing her long, silky hair when the phone rang. "Mike, I'm so glad you called!"

"So am I. I'm going to be leaving the country this afternoon and hoped I'd be able to catch you in so I'd have a chance to say good-bye."

Concern crept into Kate's voice. "It has something to do with the attempt on your life, doesn't it? I just hope you're not in over your head."

Anderson let her question go unanswered. "I have some things I want to say, so please let me talk. I'm a changed man. I know that sounds hackneyed, even corny, but when it happens to you it isn't trite at all, it's just the opposite. Really quite profound. I never thought I'd let myself feel this way again. But, fortunately, I was mistaken. Life looks different to me now, in several ways, some of which you've probably noticed by my actions, others I'll tell you when I return from my, uh, trip.

"Even thinking about being alone is different. Not that I mind it particularly. But, before, I wouldn't have thought of it as something I might like or dislike. Before, I always prefered being alone to being with others. Now, that never seems to be the case. I'd always rather be with you." Anderson stopped, the spontaneity of his words catching him by surprise. "I'm going to have to change the subject. Hearing my words are making me nervous. As I said before, I'll be gone for a while. A few days, perhaps longer. Right now, there's just no way I can tell. That's the worst part, not knowing when I'll see you again. But, when I do, believe me, I'm not going to let you out of my sight, and I don't mean for a day or two. I mean for years. I want you to know how happy I am when I picture your face, your voice. I never dreamt I was meant to experience these feelings."

"Mike. Please be careful." Suddenly Kate was caught by an uncontrollable impulse, one she couldn't contain. She had to let the words out, regardless of their effect. "I love you so."

"Me too. Me too."

Twenty-six

NEVER BEFORE HAD PEG RUSSELL EXPERIENCED SUCH conflicting emotions. A phone call from a man presumed dead had sent her mind reeling. Any relief in learning Anderson was alive was overshadowed by the tenor of his voice, the context of his words.

Anderson's accusations enraged her. Why was he trying to scare her about John and also defame her lover's character? Nobody knew McCormick better than she. They'd shared everything for years. Peg knew that she loved McCormick and he loved her, and she wasn't going to let any doubts creep in to confuse her.

Peg had promised Anderson a plane would be ready at the National Airport for a four o'clock takeoff and a car waiting in Lucerne. A promise was a promise. She owed him; she'd deliver. But, Peg thought to herself, that was all she'd do. She wasn't about to let Anderson play with her mind.

Suddenly Peg was struck by an idea, a thought that erased all remnants of anger. Anderson had unwittingly done her a favor. Peg had wanted to go with John to the summit, partly out of concern for her husband, but primarily to have time to be alone with McCormick. However, Peg had misjudged John's response to her request. The president had insisted she stay in Washington, that he'd be busy and she'd have nothing to do. She pressed, he resisted, and eventually the issue was dropped.

How ironic, Peg mused, that she'd be going along to Lucerne after all.

She walked to Russell's desk, opened the top drawer, and pulled out the papers relating to the summit. Rummaging through the papers, she quickly found the location where the president was staying: St. Le Crems #5, Seelesberg. Phone: 206-27-23.

Peg reached for the telephone on the desk. She'd call Russell, tell him Anderson was alive, wanted to be present at the summit in case his friend needed help, insisted Peg accompany him, and that they'd be leaving in a few hours.

She was certain once her husband knew Mike was alive he'd be filled with renewed energy and determination and pleased that they were coming.

Suddenly she stopped dialing, her thoughts shifting gear to McCormick. Her heart began pounding in anticipation of seeing him. John could wait. She wanted to contact Art, to let him know about her plans.

Quickly, Peg rang up Western Union and began dictating her communiqué. *"Art, Anderson's alive. Believes John's in imminent danger. Set to fly to Switzerland this afternoon. Arrive Lucerne 8 A.M. We'll see you in Seelesberg. Peg."*

She replaced the receiver and smiled to herself. She'd have given anything to be able to see the look on McCormick's face when he read the Telex.

No possibilities overlooked, all contingencies weighed. A foreigner speaking a strange dialect in a secluded corner of the world expecting the worst had to be prepared for every eventuality, Anderson thought as he placed three vials of Adrenalin, several syringes equipped with needles, and his stethoscope into his suitcase. He then glanced in the direction of his gun collection. Was he seriously considering taking a gun on this trip? He was a doctor, not a secret agent. However, he'd inadvertently found himself playing in the wrong league, the league of secret agents, and to do so and succeed, he'd have to play it their way, with their rules. He had no other choice.

Anderson felt his muscles tighten as he opened the cabinet doors and began selecting a gun. This time not for sport but to ensure survival.

His eyes scanned the assortment of weapons, each gun neatly arranged according to type. The historical pieces, those priceless fifteenth-century matchlock guns of which he was the proud owner of three and his two sixteenth-century rifled wheel locks that ushered in the era of target shooting. Next to the antique pieces was his practical arsenal, a row of revolvers followed by a row of automatics. His eyes examined each gun, his mind methodically eliminating those not suited to his purpose.

Anderson lifted the Magnum 357 perched next to his Smith & Wesson chief special barrel revolver, paused for a moment, checked to ensure the chambers were empty, and pulled the trigger. The cylinder revolved, bringing a fresh chamber in line with the hammer, locking the cylinder in place. The hammer was now in position to discharge a cartridge. Satisfied with the workings of the weapon, he reached into a drawer, pulled out several bullets, and fed them into their respective chambers.

He forced the revolver into an elongated holster held in place above his waist by a wide belt, the handle of the powerful Magnum protruding from the outside leather case. Attached to the barrel, Anderson placed an added appendage, a perforated cylinder, a silencer. He felt the uncomfortable pressure of the large revolver beneath his belt.

He paced the living room, eyed the remaining guns in the cabinet, and continued pacing. Anderson felt more secure with the weight of the revolver around his midsection, but somehow it wasn't enough. He moved back to the cabinet, pulled out a police special automatic from its lodgings, stared at the energy recoil mechanism that would activate the gun, and after a moment's hesitancy filled the magazine located in the butt of the pistol with cartridges.

Anderson forced the automatic into the inside pocket of his jacket. The snub-nosed police special was a short piece, easily concealed, while the Magnum with its attached silencer could be advantageous in circumstances demanding an absence of sound. There were just too many variables, too many unknowns to contend with. Deciding to keep both weapons eased Anderson's apprehension. He was now set.

Anderson snapped his suitcase shut and called for a taxi. If everything followed schedule, he'd be at LaGuardia within the hour, and at National by one. That would give him ample time to get to Peg. The rest depended on her.

McCormick gulped hard, his teeth clenched as he finished reading Peg's telegram, crushed it into a small ball, and heaved it into the brick fireplace. A mixture of shock, anger, and fear overcame him. He'd been certain Steele had killed Anderson.

His mind raced back into time, back to when things were simpler. He and Peg in love, no concerns for where things were headed. Now, suddenly everything had been altered. A plan that had taken years to nurture was thrown out of control by an overzealous doctor. Anderson had to be intercepted before he reached Russell. Intercepted and killed. That decision was an easy one. To reconcile his love for Peg with his loyalty and devotion to the Soviet Union was a far more difficult matter, but personal feelings had to be excluded from his decision. His allegiance lay with his country. Those feelings had to take precedence over his love for Peg . . . even if that meant killing her.

Peg Russell preceded Anderson up the steps into the waiting 707.

She'd requested the private jet from her father. He'd complied, no questions asked. Peg had ensured the secrecy of their mission by calling on two Secret Service agents with pilot's licenses to command the plane.

Within minutes, the door slammed shut, the passenger steps were removed and the plane's lights winked as the Boeing released its wheelbrakes and swung around to face the taxi strip. The 707's engines came to full power, one at a time. Then, with all brakes released, it soared into the air.

Peg looked at Anderson and said, "Are you satisfied?"

The doctor nodded.

Peg continued. "Wait until we get to Seelesberg. You'll see how wrong you've been about McCormick. He's not the kind of man you insist he is. He'd never bury himself in a hostile country and live there for most of his life without once being contacted by those who sent him."

"Who said he hasn't been routinely in contact with Moscow?"

"That's absurd! If you knew him," Peg halted abruptly. She wasn't about to give Anderson fuel with which to cheapen their relationship.

Anderson coaxed, "Go on."

"Art worries about everything. He'd constantly be afraid that his superiors had forgotten him. What if those that initially sent him died? What you've been saying doesn't mesh with the man I know. The man I love."

Anderson inwardly bristled at Peg's naiveté but realized that until recently he had been no different. "There are always files," he said, shaking off his irritation. "It's impossible that any foreign service, let alone the KGB, would lose track of one of its sleepers, even by accident. I've spoken with Wilkinson at the State Department. He assured me the Soviet Union's agents are placed with extreme care. The fruit to be produced by McCormick's long period of gestation—a Russian coup at the summit—is the sweetest life bears."

Peg lifted herself from her seat and glanced at her watch. Let Anderson think what he wanted. She was content in the knowledge that soon she'd be where she wanted to be. Safe and secure with McCormick.

Twenty-seven

The stale air, still thick with cigarette smoke from last evening's meeting, coupled with the dampness in the room hampered Russell's breathing as he greeted the Russian premier. "I trust you had a restful sleep."

"I most certainly did. And you?"

"I'd have preferred a few more hours, but there was too much left to accomplish in the time frame allotted, so"—the president shrugged—"let's continue."

Russell marveled at the Soviet leader from across the mahogany table, and not just for his command of the English language. Molonyn's gait, more lively than he'd expected from the premier's portly figure, his cherubic face with blue ball-bearing eyes, topped by a mass of hair that managed to stay darker than the years normally permitted. The premier emanated vigor and vitality, qualities the president no longer possessed.

"Premier Molonyn," Russell began in earnest, "last night we discussed generalities. I acknowledge it was important for me to hear your views and you to listen to mine. But, in our discussion on the deployment of missiles, as well as on our talk concerning the use of black boxes to detect nuclear tests, we only managed to scratch the surface. If we're to break new ground, let alone reach our goal at these meetings, both of us had better get down to specifics."

Molonyn nodded in agreement. "In 1981, the Soviet Union proposed a complete ban on all space weapons. But at the time perhaps we were too rigid in insisting that if another nation launched antisatellite weapons in space then we'd renounce any agreements reached and renew our space efforts. The USSR is now willing to assure the commitment, not to put into outer space any type of antisatellite weapon, unless your nation reneges on her commitment."

A smile swept across the president's face. "Premier Molonyn, if your country's philosophy on each of the matters before us is as flexible as that which you've just elucidated then I feel optimistic that when we leave Rutli Sunday evening, we'll have accomplished our purpose. The United States, on her part, wants it known that like our 1983 grain deal with your nation, we are prepared to guarantee via a written clause that under no condition will these agreements be canceled."

"Sounds reasonable, Mr. President. Let's get on to the next matter," Molonyn replied, leaning forward in his chair and glancing at the papers laid out in front of him.

A bald, heavyset man opened the door carrying two breakfast trays.

In the outer room, McCormick and Russell's Secret Service contingent were having an animated conversation. The sound of their voices distracted the president, his coffee spilling to the floor.

Molonyn, observing, said nothing.

They ate in relative silence. The premier, on occasion lifting his head, carefully monitored Russell's movements.

The house for their meetings had been selected by Molonyn. It was a stone building with primitive features, communication between stories only possible through outside stairs and wooden galleries, the windows in the upper gable left open, creating a draft. Cool, damp air added to the president's discomfort.

Molonyn spoke. "It's best we resume. Too much food is bad for the mind."

A moment passed. Russell didn't reply.

"Mr. President, let's continue."

"Oh, yes, ah, by all means." The president finally answered. What the hell had happened? Why hadn't he responded when Molonyn initially spoke? He'd heard every word but . . . Russell became gripped by fear. He had to settle down. There was no reason to panic. Hadn't McCormick assured him everything would be fine? The president took a deep breath, attempting to regain his composure.

"Are you all right?" Molonyn asked, feigning concern.

"Yes, I'm fine. What issue's next?"

"Last night you demanded we direct our attention to the matter of the black boxes."

Russell looked puzzled, his anxiety returning. He didn't recall that part of their discussion. Quickly he looked through his notes. He had to organize his thoughts logically, present his arguments firmly. A critical topic demanded strength and convictions. Dammit! He'd followed McCormick's orders perfectly. Why then was something going wrong?

Slowly the mist cleared. The confusion receded. A sense of elation filled him. Whatever happened had passed. He rushed in, seizing the moment. "We've got to come up with a network for monitoring a comprehensive nuclear test ban. Up to now seismologists have had to rely on seismic stations, the so-called black boxes already planted throughout the world to detect when a P wave has occurred, signifying that energy in the form of a nuclear test has taken place."

Molonyn sat still, patiently listening. Russell continued, "Both your country and mine have learned how to disguise these tests. We detonate explosions in large cavities within salt deposits. This technique effectively muffles the shock waves."

"And your proposal, Mr. President?"

"It's far too easy to conduct these tests without the black boxes picking them up. Their numbers are far too few to be effective and those that do exist have frequently been placed in locations far too remote from the test site to be of use. What I propose would be a network of fifteen stations inside the Soviet Union as well as fifteen stations outside your country."

Molonyn, startled, replied, "That's out of the question!"

"Our scientists have insisted that there's no alternative. Anything short of what I've outlined won't work. Naturally, the United States is prepared to follow suit and build fifteen stations within our country in mutually agreed-on locations."

The premier's position remained firm. "I repeat. I can't go along with what you're proposing."

Russell's impatience grew. "I was under the impression everything was negotiable. That we're here to put the past behind us. To do that demands flexibility."

Molonyn broke in, "On both our parts, Mr. President."

"What about our insistence that we be given on-site inspection of these sites at our discretion?"

"Mr. President," the premier said pounding his fist on the table, "you're being as stubborn and rigid as you're accusing me of being. I agree we've got to be flexible during these meetings, or we'll get nowhere."

Russell waited a moment, letting the tension subside before speaking. "What is the Soviet Union's counterproposal?"

"No more than fifteen stations in total, five of which we'll agree to have placed within our country, and no on-site inspection."

"In that case, what guarantees do we have that the Soviet Union will not continue nuclear tests?"

"Trust, Mr. President," Molonyn whispered, "nothing but trust. After all, isn't that what everything comes down to in the end?"

Suddenly Russell was seized by a knifelike sensation that ripped through his brain, its intensity momentarily blinding him. He pressed his hands tightly around his head, desperately trying to stop the agony.

The throbbing pain continued, tearing through his system, forcing him to gag.

The pain intolerable, his head about to explode, Russell had to summon McCormick. He tried calling out. Nothing. Silence. Words wouldn't come. The realization that he was unable to talk enveloped him with fear. He was about to die and helpless to prevent it.

Then, as suddenly and mysteriously as the attack began, it ended.

Russell turned toward the closed door. "McCormick, McCormick!" he screamed.

The pain gone, the president looked at the Russian premier. Was it possible that Molonyn had not seen what he had just gone through?

Molonyn excused himself and went to the outer room.

McCormick rushed into the conference room. After checking Russell's vital signs, he plunged the syringe filled with ten milligrams of morphine sulfate into the president's right arm. "You'll be fine, Mr. President. Give the medication five minutes to work."

"Art, what's happened?"

"I don't know, but try not to worry. I gave you my word that I'd see you successfully through these meetings. I'm not going to let you down."

Russell eyed the doctor. For the first time, McCormick's words didn't reassure him. There was something wrong, terribly wrong, something that medication could not solve.

Slowly Russell felt his apprehension lessen, a new surge of energy developing. Perhaps McCormick was right. Maybe the medication was all that was needed.

McCormick left, and the premier reentered the room. The president gazed at Molonyn, calmly exhaling white clouds of smoke. "Refresh my memory. Where were we?"

Molonyn, tasting victory, was quick to respond. "We had agreed on limiting the number of seismic stations to a total of fifteen."

The president looked puzzled. Russell knew the United States seismologists insisted on thirty stations as the absolute minimum needed, yet Molonyn insisted they had agreed on only fifteen.

Russell felt lost, confused. Not being able to remember what had taken place in their negotiations before the onset of his headache infuriated him.

He needed time to be alone, to rest, to try to regain some semblance of control. Too much was at stake to continue the summit now. He had to wait until his memory returned, until he was able to recall what had actually gone on.

Russell stood up, his gait unsteady. "Let's stop until this afternoon."

"That's not a good idea. We've got so much to accomplish and so little time in which to do it."

"You're right, but I don't see where I have a choice. I'm not up to continuing."

The premier looked at his watch. "It's now ten-fifteen. What do you suggest?"

"Reconvene at two."

Molonyn threw up his arms in disgust. "I only hope that will give us enough time."

"If we work together, we'll have more than enough time."

"Not if your health gives out."

"It won't. Believe me, it won't. A short nap, and I'll be

fine," Russell replied. His tone was confident, masking his inner doubt.

"Cullie, it's Bart."

"How are you all?" the Senate majority leader asked, chomping on a wet cigar butt. "Have you heard from Russell?"

"That's why I'm calling. I just got off the phone with McCormick. He assured me all's going well. The president's mentally sharp, alert, and handling himself well."

"That's mighty good to hear. I'll pass the news to the other members of the committee. They'll all be relieved."

"So am I, Cullie. So am I."

Twenty-eight

THE BLACK RENAULT CAME TO AN ABRUPT HALT. KURtin, the taller of the two Secret Service agents, got out of the car and opened the rear door; Peg Russell and Anderson climbed into the back seat.

It was 11:23 A.M. They were late. Severe turbulence had held up their landing for fifty-five minutes. The clouds which had been massing over the lake region had burst apart, drenching the area with rain. A brisk wind wrestled with the trees and a bolt of lightning followed by a clap of thunder greeted the car as it threaded its way from the airport into town.

Hale, the driver, suddenly swung the car sharply to the left; an uprooted tree was blocking their path. The rain bore down on the hood with increasing force, the visibility poor. Anderson realized the long trip ahead was going to be more than difficult. With the elements against them, it was going to be nearly impossible.

The Renault skidded slightly on the slick roadway as it headed south into the hills beyond Lucerne. Fog rolling in from the lake blanketed the windshield. Hale flipped on the headlights, their effect minimal.

Anderson felt the car accelerating, looked at Hale, the driver's right foot placed hard on the accelerator, his left foot grazing the brakes, waiting for those instants when balance would be in jeopardy.

Why the sudden increase in speed? Their plane had been delayed. Anderson thought that perhaps Hale was trying to make up for lost time. But, the doctor realized, if that was the case, then Hale would have driven at this rate since leaving the airport. He hadn't. Not until now. "What's up?" Anderson blurted out. "Why the speed?"

"Turn around. See for yourself."

Anderson looked. Lights. Wide white beams through the angry diagonal sheets of rain were discernible.

"It's a Fiat. Been behind us since we left the airport," Hale said. "After we entered the mountain passes, it's been creeping closer. It's obviously following us."

Anderson's pulse began racing. He hadn't told anybody they were flying to Lucerne. Nobody knew about this trip. Nobody but . . . Peg. He tried to brush aside the thought. It didn't make sense. Unless . . . Anderson was about to confront her when a bullet ricocheted off their trunk, followed by a second that shattered the outside mirror.

Kurtin turned to Mrs. Russell. "Quick, get down on the floor."

Without further words, Kurtin climbed into the back seat.

"Anderson," Kurton barked, throwing him an automatic. Mike grabbed the weapon.

"I hope you know how to use this."

Anderson nodded. This wasn't the time to tell Kurtin he had two of his own guns with him. That would only arouse unnecessary suspicion. He'd keep still, use the government's weapon, save his for later. Silently he wondered if they'd survive this ambush so there would be a later.

Hale floored the engine, the grinding gears strained, and the tires under them shrieked to a crescendo. He held the wheel with all his strength, careening into each turn, the Fiat keeping pace . . . gaining.

"They're trying to overtake us," Hale shouted. "Hold on."

Bullets being fired rapidly, repeatedly from behind them, echoed throughout the mountains.

Peg screamed out, "We're going to be killed."

Anderson glared at her, saying nothing.

"Dammit," Kurtin yelled, opening up his rear window, "I'm going to open fire. I don't know who they are, but they mean business."

The Secret Service agent took careful aim at the approaching vehicle. His target was its radiator. Pellets of rain hindering his view, the bullet missed its mark and embedded itself into the car's fender.

Undismayed, the trained bodyguard's instincts raced back into action. He fired again, puncturing the left front tire. Kurtin, wasting no time, aimed this time at the right front wheel. The impact sudden, the car went out of control, spinning. The fourth bullet exploded directly into the Fiat, fracturing the windshield, fragments of glass flying into the menacing faces behind it.

Screams of agony were heard in the distance. With no one at the wheel the car smashed into the concrete embankment. Then silence.

"That was a close call. What the hell was that all about?" Hale asked bewilderedly, wiping sweat from his brow.

Anderson's eyes turned to Peg's.

She sat still, her mind ravaged by confusion.

"Do you believe me now? They knew we were coming. We were sitting ducks."

She squirmed restlessly in her seat.

Anderson continued, "Did you tell McCormick we were coming here?"

Peg hesitated briefly. "Yes," she whispered.

"What did you tell him?"

The first lady sighed deeply. "I sent him a Telex informing him of our plan and when we'd be arriving."

Anderson's anger surfaced. "Are you satisfied now! McCormick was willing to kill you in order to stop me. What other evidence do you need?"

"I know McCormick. He wouldn't do this. There's got to be another explanation. There's just got to be."

"There is none," Anderson replied sharply.

Steve Kurtin put his automatic down and gave Hale the gun he'd given Anderson to use. "We're in the clear, at least for now. It doesn't look like they had a backup." He moved up to his seat. "Stan, put a move on. The doc here's got to get to the president . . . and fast."

Twenty-nine

Each breath an effort, every movement exhausting, his head felt as though it was caught in an evertightening vise. He'd rested for two hours. Why then was the mist returning? Why weren't the symptoms lifting? He had no energy left to tolerate them. Somehow he had to push these thoughts out of his mind and summon the strength to continue.

Russell glanced at his radium dial: one-twelve. The summit was set to resume in less than an hour. The president sat in bed, moved his legs quietly over the side, and rose slowly to his feet. It was important to refrain from any sudden movement, any jarring noise, anything that might worsen his already weakened state.

McCormick walked over to him. "Mr. President, we'd better get a move on," he said softly.

"I'm a bit dizzy. It feels as if the room's spinning."

"That sometimes happens after suddenly awakening from a deep sleep. It's nothing to be alarmed about. It'll pass," McCormick replied, his tone calm, his manner reassuring. "Need any help getting dressed?"

"No, that's okay. I can manage," Russell said, walking toward the closet.

McCormick kept his eyes riveted on the president. His gait was unsteady, his imbalance apparent.

Something was indeed going on inside Russell's brain, something McCormick hadn't counted on, something that threatened to destroy not only the president but the plans of the Soviet Union: plans predicated on Russell's signature, his name affixed to documents he and Molonyn had yet to draft.

It was imperative he calm Russell down, inspire him to continue, propel him to Rutli. The treaties had to be drawn up and signed. After that, thought McCormick, nature could take its course. Whatever was ticking away within the president's head could then safely explode.

"I don't think I can make it," Russell said, his eyes registering defeat.

"You can. Lean on me. I'll get you through," McCormick said.

Russell turned and faced the doctor. "Yes, but at what cost?"

"You can't give up now. You've lived for this day, to put an end to nuclear war. You've come so far. Believe me, you've got the stamina to make it."

Russell clumsily pushed his right leg through his trousers. He wanted to believe, had to believe McCormick. He wouldn't cancel the meetings. They were too important. He hoped to God his decision was right.

They kept winding their way alongside the lake, climbing upwards. Since Stans, the road had narrowed, become steeper, even more tortuous.

"Isn't the rain ever going to let up?" Kurtin asked as he navigated the Renault through the resort village of Beckenried.

The three passengers sat in silence, deep in thought, not

knowing what awaited them in Seelesberg. The car sped through the village of Emetten, along the slopes of the Klewenstock, past a flooded meadowland, and then through a forest. Two miles later, they glided through a tunnel, the Hotel Sonnenberg appearing on the right, two hundred yards later St. Le Crems Number Five on the left . . . a farmhouse, its present tenant—the Presidential party.

"I don't believe the spot they've chosen," Hale said, nodding his head in dismay. "I just hope it's smooth sailing from here on in. I'd hate like hell to have to get out of here in a hurry."

Anderson faced the agent. "Don't count on it."

Kurtin looked up. "I know it's our job to defend the president and his family. Risk our own lives if necessary. Never questioning, just obeying orders. So if I'm out of line, tell me to shut up, but I'd love to know what the hell is going on. I'm asked to fly a private jet to Lucerne. We get to Switzerland, have a greeting party waiting for our arrival, a welcoming committee of hunters that view us as prey. Fill in the gaps, Anderson, will you!"

Anderson hesitated briefly. The agent's logic was undeniable. He needed their help, and they deserved some information.

Anderson told the essential parts of the incredible story. He finished as Kurtin eased the car to a halt one hundred yards past the farmhouse, in a clearing safely off the road.

Kurtin was silent behind the wheel. Hale frowned, "We'd better get to the house right away." He looked at the doctor, "You're not experienced in taking these kinds of risks. You won't know what to do. It's best if Steve and I take over from here. You and Mrs. Russell stay here until we get McCormick out of the way. Then you can safely go in and see the president."

Anderson, alarmed, answered, "No! That's not a good idea.

The president very likely wouldn't be able to handle the shock of seeing two of his Secret Service agents barge in unexpectedly like that and drag McCormick out. I'm afraid that could be the final straw. The stress could kill him."

Kurtin turned and faced Peg. "Mrs. Russell, what do you think?"

Peg sat still, blood drained from her face.

"Please, Mrs. Russell. We've got to get into that house. We need your answer."

"Peg," Anderson shook her. "Peg. Hurry. Answer them."

Finally, she responded, "The doctor's right. My husband is better off if we are the ones to greet him, at least initially."

Anderson smiled, "Thanks, Peg. Maybe you're finally seeing the light."

Hale opened his door. "Come on, let's go. We'll stay outside the house. But promise us one thing, at the first sign of trouble, holler. That's what we're paid for. Just yell and we'll be there."

Anderson and Peg nodded in agreement as they climbed out of the car and raced down the hill, to the brick farmhouse . . . and Russell. Anderson felt the gun in his belt and the other in his jacket; they were secure.

The grass was beaded with moisture. Anderson led Peg to the old house down a path bordered by flowers, past the stone wall, remnants of a fourteenth-century monastery. They approached the house and stood in front of the ancient cottage. It was eerily still. Somewhere within were Russell and McCormick.

Russell reached across the desk, grabbed his attaché case in his right hand, and, gripping it tightly, said to McCormick, who was standing by the closed bedroom door, "I'm ready. Just keep your fingers crossed."

Without warning, the room began spinning, Russell's body

swayed back and forth. The president looked for a nearby wall to brace himself, to prevent falling to the floor.

A harsh buzzing sound, unexpected, reverberated through his head, its pitch intensifying, the noise transformed into a deafening roar.

The significance was obvious to Russell. He called out, "Art, I'm having another attack."

McCormick rushed to his medical bag, pulled out two large white tablets, ran to the bathroom, filled the glass with water, and dashed back to find the president seated in a chair, looking disoriented, the right side of his face twisted almost beyond recognition. Desperately trying to control his mounting panic, McCormick took several deep breaths and in as calm a voice as possible said, "Here, Mr. President, take these. They'll stop the attack."

Russell reached for the glass and, with his hand trembling, brought it to his mouth. Within seconds, an explosive cough pierced the air, he regurgitated the two tablets. He tried swallowing them again. The result was identical. His throat no longer could perform its function.

He stared at McCormick in growing terror.

Then the pounding started, softly at first, within minutes building to a crescendo, initially behind his left temple, rapidly spreading to encompass his entire head. It felt as if hammers were being smashed against his skull by some madman. The pain was excruciating, unbearable.

McCormick quickly injected twenty-five milligrams of Demerol, a potent painkiller, into the president's left arm. Two minutes later, the pain eased sufficiently for Russell to catch his breath.

"Art, what is it?" he uttered, the words slurred, hard to decipher.

McCormick, perspiration rolling down his face, looked at his watch: 1:38 P.M. He had to come up with something, anything to get the president back on his feet. He sensed his control collapsing.

In desperation, McCormick lifted Russell from his chair. The president stood still, motionless.

"I'll help you," the doctor cried out, "give me your arm."

The president went to drape his right arm over McCormick's broad shoulders. Nothing. The arm wouldn't move. It was dead. He felt like a puppeteer helplessly pulling on the string, the marionette not moving.

McCormick assisted the president back to his chair. "I'm sorry," Russell said, the words garbled, the right side of his mouth drooping.

McCormick frantically paced the room, preoccupied, oblivious to the paralysis that had begun to creep up Russell's right leg.

Anderson tried to keep his breathing controlled as he mounted the steps, Peg trailing behind.

He reached the second floor landing, stood there for an interminable moment, listening for any sound of footsteps or voices in the hall. Nothing, except the beat of his heart.

Anderson edged his way to the closed door, the wooden panel behind which two men were housed, one whom he had come to save, who didn't know he needed saving, and the other, who thought he was safe, whom he had come to destroy.

Anderson eased the door open slightly and heard a voice. He froze instinctively. It was McCormick's voice. Then silence, followed by the doctor's voice again. He hadn't heard Russell speak. There hadn't been any response from the president. Was he already too late?

Mike couldn't wait any longer. He barged in, Peg following. McCormick came in full view. He was a bull of a man, his open shirt emphasizing the thickness of his neck and chest, the stretched clothing marking the breadth of his heavy shoulders. Anderson hadn't realized McCormick was this formidable. Once again, he felt for his guns, hoping neither weapon would be called for; words, frequently more effective, were infinitely preferable.

Anderson scanned the room, his eyes coming to rest on the president, seated in his chair, his body slumped forward. "John, it's me. Michael."

Russell summoned the energy to raise his head, his vision blurred. "Michael. I, I . . . it can't be. You're dead."

"No. I'm very much alive. Peg and I are here. Hang on. Please God, hang on."

Peg walked over to her husband's side, tears in her eyes.

"Peg, Peg, is that you? I don't understand. Everything's happening so fast."

"Yes, it's me," she said, gently stroking his head. "Please, save your strength. Don't talk."

Anderson was stunned by his friend's rapid deterioration. He had to examine the president immediately and then get him to the nearest hospital. Russell's life was on the line. He hoped McCormick wasn't totally absorbed in his objective, that he still had some human compassion, some humanity, remaining. To get urgent medical assistance demanded McCormick's cooperation.

Could he enlist the Russian's help?

The answer wasn't long in coming. Out of the corner of his eye, Michael saw McCormick dash to the desk, to his medical bag, and pull out a gun.

Like a cat operating on survival instincts alone without thought or reason, Anderson sprang at his enemy, eyes and mind and body on a single object. The gun. The barrel of the gun.

He reached it, his fingers gripping the warm steel, hand and wrist twisting counterclockwise, pulling downward to inflict the greatest pain. McCormick, to free his arm, pulled the gun by its barrel and swung it viciously. The handle of the gun caught Anderson in the temple. Searing shafts of pain caused countless white spots to converge in front of his eyes. Operating blindly, Anderson crouched down and lunged forward, smashing his head into McCormick's stomach, momentarily winding him.

Anderson righted himself, his sight returning. The gun, he had to get the gun. He jabbed his right hand, fingers curled and rigid, into the traitor's solar plexus, tearing at his muscles, feeling the protrusion of his rib cage. He yanked up with all his strength; McCormick reeling backwards, crashed into the dresser, the gun falling from his hand, to the floor. Anderson kicked it to the side, towards Peg.

The first lady bent down and grabbed the weapon. Her hands trembled. She'd never held a gun before. Her mouth quivered.

Anderson backed away, opened his jacket, the holster now accessible. As he pulled out the Magnum, McCormick leaped into the air, catching Anderson off guard and ramming his fist into his groin. The pain made Michael retch. McCormick grabbed Anderson's weapon and stood up, the barrel pointed directly at Michael's stomach.

"Stop it. Both of you stop it," Peg screamed, the gun hanging loosely by her side. What should she do? What could she do? She looked at her husband, his right arm limp, his eyes pleading. Then at Anderson, her husband's closest friend, the one who had implanted seeds of doubt in her mind. What were his intentions? Could his actions be a result of jealousy, as Art insisted? And then there was McCormick, her lover, until now her rock, her strength. Why then did he prevent Mike from examining her husband, from immediately rushing him to a hospital?

The president, in a hushed voice, barely audible, broke the

silence. "What's the fighting all about? I need help. Please, Mike. Art. Do something!"

Anderson glared at Peg. "John's right. He needs immediate medical attention or he'll die. You've got to get Art to listen."

"There's nothing to talk about," McCormick replied angrily, his finger pressed against the trigger. "Peg, I know what I'm doing. I've never let you down. I'll attend to John, but first I—we've got to get rid of Anderson. He's ruining everything."

Anderson replied, "There it is, Peg, out of his own mouth. I've ruined everything? I've ruined nothing! All I've been trying to do is save your husband. Ask him. Go ahead, ask Art. He's the one who's kept me from treating John. It's because of him your husband might die. Well, Peg, go ahead. Let's see him worm his way out of this one."

"Shut up, Anderson. Don't listen to him, Peg. Of course I'm going to take care of John, but first things first."

"Dammit, Peg," Anderson shouted. "What's more urgent than helping a dying man?"

"Shut up, both of you. You're making me so confused." Her mind was a mass of contradictions. Had she been betrayed, and if so, by whom? Who in God's name should she believe?

The president's thick voice broke in. "Peg, I don't know what's going on, but I'm dying. Trust Mike. Do as he says."

McCormick pleaded, "Peg, don't forget all of our plans. Don't throw them away. They mean too much to me."

"Don't let him con you again. He's too persuasive," Anderson cried.

Suddenly Anderson's eyes brightened. Why hadn't he noticed it before? Where a moment ago he could only see darkness, light now appeared. "If you need any more proof that I've been right all along, Peg, just look down. Take a good look at the gun in your hand. Study it carefully. It's a Graz-

Bura. It's the most powerful and accurate revolver," he paused as Peg's eyes moved downward, her hands cupping the weapon, "but it's only made in Russia."

McCormick started to approach Peg. "Give me the gun. This is getting ridiculous."

"Don't come any closer, Art. I'm all confused. Everything's happening so fast. I need time to think. To collect my thoughts."

"There's nothing to think about, Peg, believe me. Your husband's beyond salvage. Forget him. Just hand me your gun!"

"How can you say such a thing?" she replied, her scowl failing to conceal her indecision.

McCormick drew closer.

"Please, Art. Stay where you are!"

McCormick ignored her command, kept advancing. He drew within inches of her and reached out to grab her gun. A violent roar pierced the stillness, blood spurted from McCormick's chest. His body was propelled backward by the force of the bullet into a wooden table, his fingers still firmly pressed against the trigger. The sudden impact jolted his right hand, the Magnum accidentally firing. The bullet's trajectory straight ahead . . . striking Peg in the neck and ripping through her skull. She fell to the floor, the sound muted by a thick layer of carpeting, her fingers clawing at the wool, her blood-streaked face mercifully concealed. A final spasm, and all movement stopped.

Kurtin, followed by the other agents, raced through the half-open doorway. Blood drained from his face as he saw Peg. He quickly turned her body over, her skull shattered, pieces of brain visible.

Schore, another of the agents, bent over McCormick. "He's dead, too."

Russell shrieked as the reality suddenly overcame him. "Peg, Peg," he cried.

Anderson, quickly recovering, walked over to Russell, and bent down to face the president. "We've got to get you to a hospital right away."

Russell lifted his left hand into the air and pointed to the floor where Peg lay. "Mike, I might not make it to the hospital. Answer me one thing."

Anderson drew in deeply. He knew his friend well. He was certain of the question.

"What did McCormick mean by 'all of our plans.' Were they lovers?"

Mike had never intentionally deceived Russell, had never lied to his best friend. Yet what purpose would be served if John knew the truth? Perhaps Peg had meant to pull the trigger and would have redeemed herself had she lived. Either way it all seemed irrelevant, already light-years away. "She killed him. She died for you. What more do you need?"

A smile creased the president's face. Within seconds, he fell unconscious.

Mike lifted Russell to the bed and began a cursory examination. Every second counted. None could be wasted. How much longer Russell had, nobody knew.

Anderson saw the president's pupils. They were unequal and dilated, indicating an insufficient amount of oxygen was getting to his brain. He grabbed a nearby lamp, shining it into Russell's eyes. The pupils barely reacted. Another grave sign.

Quickly he lifted the president's legs, observing the left one had the proper tone while the right one was flaccid.

Anderson had to maintain his composure and stop his mounting panic. He had to come up with the cause of the president's coma. Everything depended on him.

What had suddenly erupted inside John's brain, sending him into an unconscious state?

All at once, everything came together. Anderson had the answer. A shift of the pineal gland to the right. The slow deterioration of the president's mental facilities. Everything now made sense. The mass was clearly not a tumor. Rather it was a slowly growing aneurysm; the only vessel capable of producing this cluster of symptoms, the left middle cerebral artery.

The symptoms were identical to Alzheimer's. The stress and strain of the summit caused the ballooned-out artery to explode, spilling its contents over the brain.

Anderson finally had the answer. Russell no longer faced the prospect of ending his life in a nursing home, a vegetable, or dying a slow agonizing death, the victim of a brain tumor. No, his best friend would either die within a few hours from the ruptured blood vessel, or he'd live and do so without significant impairment.

Russell's life hinged on Anderson's ability to take charge, to act rapidly. He glanced around the room, at the four Secret Service men. Kurtin and Hale, who had come with him to Seelesberg, and Keyser and Schore, who had accompanied Russell. "Where's the nearest hospital?"

Schore replied, "It's in Stans. Russell had me check on that one on our arrival. Maybe he knew more than the rest of us."

Anderson interrupted, "I know where Stans is. What are their facilities like?"

"It's a relatively modern hospital. Seventy beds. They have an intensive care unit."

"Get them on the line. Explain the situation to them"—Anderson paused briefly—"uh, tell them we've got a medical emergency, that we'll need a neurosurgeon or, if they don't have any on their staff, a surgeon who's at least done some brain surgery."

"Okay, sir." Schore was about to leave when Anderson spoke again. "One additional thing. We've got to protect the president and also avoid any unnecessary panic. Don't tell them who the patient is. Make up a name. Later on, depending on what happens, we'll decide on how and what to tell them. Now go to it."

Anderson then turned to Keyser. "What's the fastest way out of here?"

"The cable system. It covers the entire mountain range."

"Contact them. Get them to send us a car immediately."

"Sorry, sir," Keyser replied, "the weather's knocked out their lines. They can't run when the cable gets wet. It's too dangerous."

"What about the steamers then? Don't they run up and the down the lake region?"

"Yes, sir. But when the weather's like this, I'm afraid they don't run either."

"Dammit. Well then, I guess we have no alternative but to have the hospital send an ambulance. It'll be much slower, but we don't have any other choice."

Schore caught the tail end of the conversation as he reentered the room. "Forget it, doc. I asked. Stans Memorial Hospital had one ambulance. It was totaled earlier today while picking up a cardiac arrest. It skidded on the slick roads. They won't be able to get their hands on another one until tomorrow at the earliest."

"That's just great," Anderson said, pacing, his eyes fixed on the president. Russell's breathing was becoming more erratic. "Well, I guess we'll have to drive the president ourselves. I have some medical supplies in the car," Anderson stopped and looked up. "Who here knows CPR?"

Keyser answered, "I was a paramedic for two years in Nam."

"Good. Kurtin, you drive. Keyser and I will sit in the back

with Russell. Schore, you'd better come too. There's no telling what might happen. Let's go. We've got no time to waste. The president is barely alive. We can only hope he hangs in there until we get to Stans."

Thirty

UTILIZING SKILLS GATHERED DURING WEEKENDS SPENT as a car racing enthusiast, Kurtin adroitly guided the Renault, following the road as it twisted and curved through the mountains. Speed was of the essence. The faster he drove, the sooner Russell would get to Stans and the quicker he'd receive the medical help he desperately needed.

"How's the old man holding up?" Kurtin asked, eyes glued to the road.

Anderson's fists tightened against his thigh. The drive seemed interminable, but what little time they might save by Kurtin's accelerating was not worth the catastrophe of an accident. Things were precarious enough as they were. He didn't need another complication.

Throughout the trip, Russell slipped in and out of consciousness. Anderson, seated on one side, systematically checked his pulse, respiration, blood pressure, and pupil size, looked for changes that might indicate a sudden rise in pressure against his brain. Any further increase, either from bleeding or swelling, and he'd have only minutes to reverse the process before permanent damage began.

Kurtin's question finally registered. Anderson replied, "It doesn't look good. Pulse 140 and irregular, respiration 30 and shallow, blood pressure unstable, pupils equal but barely reactive."

Anderson constantly moved, checking, rechecking, attempting to arouse Russell.

The tension in the car was suffocating.

Suddenly Anderson called out, "His blood pressure is falling. Keyser, quick, open up my attaché case. Fill up one of the syringes with 5 cc's of adrenalin. Russell's pressure is too low. I've got to raise it or we're going to lose him."

Keyser handed Anderson the syringe. The doctor plunged the needle into the president's left arm.

Within seconds, Russell's color brightened, his pulse flowed, and his blood pressure rose and stabilized. The adrenalin had served its function. The rest depended on the president.

"Hang in there," Anderson said, "just a little longer. We're almost there."

A few minutes later, the Renault swung a sharp left. They had made it. They were at Stans Memorial Hospital. As relief swept over him, Anderson began to shake.

Several attendants and a nurse were on the receiving platform waiting for the patient to appear.

Carefully, Keyser and Anderson lifted Russell out of the car and onto the stretcher. As they wheeled the president to the emergency room, an attendant held a bottle of Ringers lactate while the nurse rapidly threaded a needle into one of the president's veins. She set the solution to run in at 50 cc per hour.

Anderson caught a brief glimpse of the hospital as they walked briskly through the corridor. The hallway was deserted except for a salmon-coated receptionist powdering her nose behind the desk. To her right, an impressive brass board listed the hospital's ten physicians.

Good God, Anderson thought, only ten doctors on the

entire staff. But Anderson realized Russell only needed one doctor, one top-notch experienced surgeon. He swallowed hard. Hopefully, Stans had such a physician on its medical staff.

The stretcher carrying the president wove its way across the empty receiving and triage area and headed straight for the trauma wing. Russell momentarily regained consciousness. Through a sea of hospital personnel, his eyes, peering from sunken shadows, met Anderson's. As Mike drew closer he saw a sparkle in Russell's pupils, a flicker of strength. He grabbed the president's hand. "We're at the hospital, John. You're going to be fine," Anderson said. Russell tried to smile.

A burly middle-aged white-haired man greeted the stretcher as it entered the trauma room. He briefly looked at his patient and called to the nurse, "Bromley, he needs a cutdown. Also type and cross-match for six units of whole blood. I don't know what we'll find. We'd better be prepared." The doctor looked up. "Any of you Anderson?"

"I am."

"I'm John Fletcher. Ever perform brain surgery before?"

Mike gulped. "No. Never."

"Well, now you're going to get the chance. I'm going to need an assistant, and there's no one else I can call on."

Suddenly, Fletcher screamed, "Holy shit. He's fibrillating." Instinctively, Anderson reached across Russell's neck and checked for a carotid pulse. For an instant, he thought he felt one. His spirits dashed. It was his own heart pounding through his fingertips.

With both fists, Fletcher delivered a sharp blow to the center of Russell's chest. Then he gave three deep mouth-to-mouth breaths and several quick compressions to his breastbone. Another carotid check showed nothing.

"Code ninety-nine," he yelled. "Code ninety-nine."

Fletcher and Anderson resumed their resuscitation. In fifteen seconds, two nurses burst into the room pushing the emergency crash cart.

Seconds later, the trauma room began to fill with people and machines. Fletcher inserted a short oral airway into Russell's mouth and began providing respiration with a breathing bag. Anderson continued the external cardiac compression.

An elderly nurse raced in pushing an electrocardiograph machine. Leads from the machine were strapped tightly to Russell's wrists and ankles.

Finally, a wiry young anesthesiologist, Dr. Gregory, appeared. He picked up a sealed laryngoscope and inserted its right-angle lighted blade deep into the president's throat, at the same time lifting up the base of his tongue to expose the fragile gray half-moons of his vocal chords.

"Give me a 7.02," he said to the nurse assisting at his side. The clear plastic tube, with a diameter of three-quarters of an inch, had a deflated plastic balloon wrapped just above the top. Skillfully, Gregory slipped the tube between Russell's vocal chords and down his trachea. He used a syringe to blow up the balloon, sealing the area around the tube, preventing air leaks. Then he grabbed the black Ambu breathing bag and attached it to the outside end of the tube, connecting oxygen to the bag, running in the life-sustaining element, setting the respiration to a rate of twenty-five per minute.

Anderson's eyes turned to the EKG screen, to the straight-line strokes of the stylus. There was no heartbeat. *Oh, my God, bring him back. Please.* The finely lined paper flowed from the machine, forming a jumbled pile at Fletcher's feet.

"Bromley, we've got to shock him. Get set to give him four hundred joules."

The nurse ran to the defibrillation machine, turned the dial to 400, squirted contact jelly on the two steel paddles, and handed them to Fletcher.

The doctor motioned everyone away. Then he quickly pressed one paddle along the inside of the president's left breast and the other one six inches below his left armpit. "Ready? Now!"

Fletcher depressed the red button on the top of the right-hand paddle. A dull thunk sounded as 400 joules of electricity shot through Russell's chest and through the rest of his body. His body arched rigidly for an instant, then was still. The cardiograph tracing showed no change.

Fletcher began ordering medication to be given through Russell's cut-down site. Bicarbonate to counteract the mounting lactic acid in his blood and tissue. Adrenalin to stimulate cardiac activity. No change. Another adrenalin injection followed by two more 400-joule countershocks. Still nothing. Calcium, more bicarbonate, a fourth shot. The straight-line reading persisted.

"Give me an amp of adrenalin in a cardiac needle," Fletcher ordered. The surgeon calmly used his fingers to count down four rib spaces and with the ampul of adrenalin in his other hand, plunged the 4½-inch needle attached to it straight down into Russell's chest. Dark red blood rushed into the ampul. The needle had hit its mark; it was in the president's heart.

Fletcher shot in the adrenalin. Anderson stood and watched the needle on the cardiograph. All at once the stylus began flashing up and down. There was a rhythm. A persistent regular rhythm. *By God, he's brought him back.* The regular rhythm continued. Fletcher backed away from the stretcher and wiped the sweat from his forehead.

"He's still with us. Let's get him to the O.R. and STAT!"

The operating room hummed with the latest technological equipment, reassuring Anderson. He peered over his surgical mask and glanced around the room, his eyes momentarily riveted on the electronic blip trace of the cardiac monitor. Russell's heart rhythm remained strong and regular.

Dr. Gregory, the anesthesiologist, checked the gauge pressure on both cylinders of oxygen hanging from the sides, waiting in the wings to be used if an emergency developed. They were fully charged. Gregory nodded his approval. He motioned to Dr. Fletcher, "You can begin."

With a saw blade, Fletcher deftly cut around the shaven skull slightly above ear level and lifted off the skullcap. Under the cold white fluorescent light, the membrane sacs containing the brain glistened. Cutting them open, he worked his rubber gloves under the frontal lobe of the brain, blindly feeling his way through the gray matter.

Fletcher barked, "Anderson, pull harder on those retractors, will you! . . . Still harder! . . . That's good. Blood is oozing from down below. The problem's coming from somewhere deeper. This man has a bleeder."

The chief surgeon sucked out several blood clots with a suction machine, the area becoming noticeably clearer. "Ah, that's better. Now we can see what we're doing."

Fletcher slowly, deliberately pushed aside portions of the gray matter, his fingers digging deeper, blindly, within the far recesses of Russell's brain.

"Anderson, you're losing your grip. I need more space. Pull harder."

Michael pulled as hard as he could. He'd never witnessed or assisted a neurosurgical procedure before. It was hard to believe the strength it took to keep the operative area clear, to keep the parts of the brain separated. He'd have more respect for his surgical associates from now on.

For a few moments Fletcher rooted around blindly. Suddenly he announced in a booming voice, "I've got the culprit. It's in my hand. Anderson, take a look," Fletcher said, pointing to a medium-sized blood vessel near the parietal lobe, "there's the little devil. Thought you'd kill our patient. No sir. We've got you." Fletcher turned toward Anderson and continued. "You had it diagnosed accurately. An aneurysm of the left middle cerebral artery affecting the dominant hemisphere. You got him here just in time. Looks like she was about to blow. Another fifteen minutes, and your friend wouldn't have made it."

The scrub nurse handed Fletcher the catgut sutures. He quickly tied off both the proximal and distal ends of the artery, clipped the ballooned outsection of the vessel and then skillfully anastomosed the two ends.

"Give me some more suction. I want to make certain I tied the whole damn thing tightly. I don't want to have the patient's condition deteriorate in the middle of the night and have to go back in."

When Fletcher was satisfied all the bleeding had stopped, he turned to Anderson. "He's out of the woods. It should be smooth sailing from here on in. Would you mind closing up? My wife will have my ass if I don't get a move on. I'm late for a dinner engagement."

Same as in the States, Anderson thought to himself. "No, not at all. That'll be fine."

Anderson sat back in his chair, staring at Russell lying in bed, peacefully sleeping, the recovery room quiet save for the rhythmic clicking of the president's respirator.

Michael yawned. He was beat. It had been a grueling time. His mind flashed back to the beginning, to the bottle of Doriden and the phone call.

The macabre events of the past few months were a blur.

Russell was going to recover. He would be fine. Anderson's thoughts drifted toward Kate Robins. It was time for him to pick up the pieces of his life.

Epilogue

Epilogue

Streams of sunlight cascaded down the stained glass windows and bounced off the altar of the thirteenth-century Gothic cathedral at the foot of Mount Rigi.

Anderson took his bride's hand, nodded to the minister, turned and slowly walked down the aisle, his eyes fixed on Kate, magnificent in the long white-lace bridal gown that had been worn for three generations by the eldest daughter in the Robins family.

The sense of hopelessness, futility, and desperation he'd learned to bear as an amputee does a prosthesis had over the past nine months gradually decreased. He still had bouts of restlessness but now they caused him to reach for Kate rather than for a pill. Unfortunately at times, memories of depression and survival were still with him. It would take more time, months, perhaps years, for them to lift completely.

The church doors opened. The sky was a deep blue; fine wisps of white clouds danced by. Switzerland in May. The persistent sun giving life to the fields, vitality to those gathered in the garden to congratulate the newlyweds. His best man, the president, fully recovered from his near-fatal hemorrhage, amicably chatting with the other guests. The only reminders of Russell's near disaster: the hairpiece needed to cover the patches of still bare scalp . . . and the absence of Peg.

How frightfully easy it had been, Anderson reflected, to feed the media what was needed to satisfy their curiosity. President and Mrs. Russell, victims of virulent bacterial food poisoning while vacationing in Europe over the Labor Day weekend. Both rushed to the nearest hospital. Peritonitis and gangrene developing. Following six hours of emergency abdominal surgery, Russell's bowel was successfully resected. His recovery painful, slow, but complete. Mrs. Russell's fate was far different, the infection spreading, overwhelming her. The surgeons unable to overcome the bacteria's onslaught. Her death on the operating room table inevitable, tragic.

Anderson had needed a liaison with the press, somebody to disseminate the story. He found his man in Henry Jackson. His name previously supplied by Eric Dawson. The reporter agreed to float the article, insisting on a photograph of the president, stomach exposed with the bandages visible. The picture visual proof to solidify the validity of their contrived story. Jackson's price for his complicity in duping the American public: ready access to the White House and advance briefings on important news developments.

Russell had agreed to the reporter's conditions. The result: a smooth transition with Kingsley at the helm until the president recovered.

Then last week, and the president's ultimate triumph. Appearing on national television, he addressed the country. His appearance strong, healthy and confident. He apologized for his long recuperative period. A period of time that ended in March. Then came the surprise announcement. He and his advisors had been meeting since March preparing for a summit conference to be held between himself and Premier Molonyn of the Soviet Union. Their objective: negotiations aimed at ending nuclear war. The date of their meeting, May 7. The place: Lucerne, Switzerland. The spot selected because of the country's ability to live for centuries in peace as well as its easy accessibility. The summit was to be beamed by satellite live around the globe.

A Gallup poll taken a day after the president's address gave Russell the greatest popularity ever accorded an incumbent prior to the start of a reelection campaign. A race Russell intended to enter and win.

Anderson looked at his bride, took her hand, and walked through the crowd. It was hard to believe how different everything was compared to the previous time he'd come to Lucerne. Rain and turmoil had blotted out all shapes and colors then. The mountains had vanished, didn't exist. Now in the sunlight, their peaks were clear and bold against the sky.

Russell tapped Anderson on the shoulder, bringing him back to the present. "Mike, I'd like a word with you." The president turned to Kate. "I need your husband for a little while. I've got a few things to talk over with Mike."

Kate smiled. "As long as this doesn't set a precedent."

Russell laughed. "Believe me, it won't. But until the summit is over, he's mine. After all, I need my personal physician with me at the meetings."

Anderson and Russell walked to the far end of the church garden, away from the noise, following a path bordered with red tulips.

"Congratulations, Mike."

"Thanks, Mr. President."

"Cut that out. In private, it's still John."

Russell, alert and fit, all weight loss regained, stared at his friend. "I'm looking forward to these next three days. We should be able to accomplish a lot. Molonyn has his back to the wall. I've made it perfectly clear to him that unless he negotiates in good faith, I'm prepared to release the true story of what went on eight months ago. To let everyone know that the Soviet Union attempted to sabotage a prearranged secret summit conference between our two countries by making certain I was in a severely weakened physical and mental state and incapable of debating with Molonyn on equal footing."

"I never knew you were an arm-twister."

Russell smiled, "There's a lot you haven't learned about me yet. I'll use anything if it'll help ram Genesis II down Molonyn's throat. If he can play dirty pool, so can I. I want a signed treaty favoring our country and I'm going to get it."

Anderson shook his head. "I guess I have a lot to learn about politics."

Russell interrupted, "About life in general, Mike. I've been telling you that since our days at Yale." The president paused. "That's enough for now. Your education's going to take quite some time. Go back to your wife. I'll meet you at the hotel in one hour. And Mike, one more thing. Thanks for joining our team."

Anderson took a deep breath, exhaled slowly, looked at his lifelong friend, then turned and began walking briskly toward Kate.

It felt good not to be totally free.